Christianity
Pure and Simple

Also by Dwight Longenecker
from Sophia Institute Press®:

Adventures in Orthodoxy

Dwight Longenecker

Christianity
Pure and Simple

SOPHIA INSTITUTE PRESS®
Manchester, New Hampshire

Sophia Institute Press®
Box 5284, Manchester, NH 03108
1-800-888-9344
www.sophiainstitute.com

Library of Congress Cataloging-in-Publication Data

Longenecker, Dwight.
Christianity pure and simple / Dwight Longenecker.
  p. cm.
Includes bibliographical references.
ISBN 1-933184-07-8 (pbk. : alk. paper)
  1. Catholic Church — Doctrines. I. Title.

BX1754.L66 2005
239 — dc22
                                2005020555

05 06 07 08 09 10 9 8 7 6 5 4 3 2 1

Contents

4. The Great Battle

5. Welcome Home

*Christianity
Pure and Simple*

Chapter One

Is Anybody There?

THE RELIGIOUS INSTINCT

Have you ever noticed that people everywhere tend to be religious? No matter where or when they have lived, the vast majority of human beings have acted on an instinct that someone else is "out there." In times of danger and in times of peace they have paused to ask for protection or to give thanks for blessings. When faced with the awesome force of nature or the miracle of a newborn child, they have looked beyond themselves to a greater power. This shared instinct has caused people throughout history to come together and establish religions.

In every society and culture, from the most primitive to the most sophisticated, people have told stories about gods, built temples, established rituals, and honored men and women they thought were particularly holy. Whether tribal people living in the jungle or sophisticated city-dwellers, simple peasants or educated scientists, most human beings at all times and in all places have worshiped some kind of divine being.

Today, no less than in times past, the signs of this religious instinct are everywhere. Walk around most any town or city, and every time you turn a corner, you will see some kind of church or religious meeting hall. Travel across the world, and you find that all the greatest monuments and buildings have religious purpose.

Christianity Pure and Simple

Everywhere you come across temples and shrines of every shape and kind, from Stonehenge to St. Peter's Basilica, from a simple Baptist church to the temples of Angkor Wat, from the ruins of a makeshift shrine in a cell at Auschwitz to the Parthenon, Chartres Cathedral, or a Buddhist pagoda.

In a multitude of fascinating, bewildering, and strange ways human beings have been driven by their religious instinct. The religious instinct has driven both individuals and empires, and has produced the greatest literature, art, architecture, and music the world has ever seen.

So, this religious instinct isn't just a quirk of one group of people; it's virtually universal among human beings. This instinct is so common to humanity that we can say it is an integral part of our nature — that being religious is as natural to human beings as swimming is to fish.

Because it is a universal human phenomenon, we have to ask ourselves what it means. Why is it that virtually all human beings everywhere have believed in some sort of God? I think that this is pretty strong evidence that there must be a God of some sort. If everyone gets thirsty, there must be such a thing as water.

Something New and Strange

Although this religious instinct can be found everywhere and in all times down through human history, in relatively recent years something strange has developed: large groups of people have come to disbelieve that there is a God. This modern phenomenon of widespread atheism is almost unique in human history, but because we are so used to it today, we don't realize how strange it is.

In our society, for all sorts of reasons, ordinary people have been taught — by their parents, their schools, their governments — not to believe in the existence of God. Therefore, before we can discuss religion, we are forced to explain why we actually believe God exists in the first place.

To the believer this is a tricky exercise. It is a bit like trying to explain the existence of love to someone who has never been in love. You might argue for love in intellectual terms. You might explain what it is like to be in love, but you would feel that you were always missing the point. You would feel that you were using intellectual language for something that is much bigger than just clever ideas and arguments. The words you used would sound awkward and inadequate. Furthermore, even if you were to convince the person who doesn't believe in love that such a thing as love exists, he still wouldn't understand what it's like to be in love. Your effort wouldn't really succeed. You would end up frustrated and think the whole exercise wasn't worth the bother.

Nevertheless, even though such explanations can take us only so far, we must start with the reasons we believe there is a God at all. Such explanations are like the instruction you have to take before an exciting sport like water skiing or skydiving. You're always tempted to skip the training and get on with the real thing. But without the training you might make critical mistakes. The basic training lays necessary foundations, and we skip it at our peril.

Do Atheists Exist?

I said just a moment ago that almost all people throughout history have believed in a God of some sort.

"Wait a minute!" you might reply. "Don't forget about the atheists."

It's a good point. Atheists don't believe God exists. But I don't believe *atheists* exist. What I mean is, even the most atheistic person lives for something. And unless he is a totally depraved and wicked person, he lives for something he believes is good.

Maybe he is passionate about truth and spends his life exposing fakes and searching for truth. Although he denies that there is a God, perhaps the atheist spends his whole life pursuing justice and peace. Or perhaps some atheists live for love. Even if they flit from one boyfriend or girlfriend to another, deep down they are looking for a love that will last forever. Maybe the atheist lives only for what he thinks is "the good life" — in other words, for his own personal pleasure. But even that is good in a way, simply because it gives him pleasure, which is good. His pursuit of pleasure also shows that he believes there is such a thing as real happiness. It's true that his pursuit of pleasure may lead him to behave selfishly. But even so, he is still, at the very basic level, living his life in the pursuit of something he believes is good.

If most "atheists" live their lives seeking something good, then they believe in something good, and if they believe in something good — something so good that they are willing to work hard to get it — then in a way they are worshiping a god. Compared with the God of religious people, the atheist's god is a very little god, and a god of their own making, but it is still a god, because it is a source of goodness outside themselves.

The Caveman and the Stars

So this desire to live for something good that is greater than ourselves is part of the universal human religious instinct. But why should this religious instinct be there at all? How did we develop this idea that there is something good worth living for, or some great being out there that we ought to worship?

Some people believe it is simply a matter of how we evolved. The caveman, they suggest, looked up at the sun, the moon, and the stars and was filled with wonder and fear at their greatness. He heard the thunder, saw the lightning, and imagined that some great being like him lived in the clouds. He imagined that this being was sometimes angry and sometimes pleased, because sometimes he blessed the man with rain and sunshine and other times punished him with drought and disaster. The caveman concluded that this being on the other side of the clouds needed to be satisfied and kept happy, and all the rest of religion, with its complicated doctrines, rules, and rituals, started to evolve.

Do you notice how this argument makes certain assumptions about cavemen? It treats the caveman as a noble savage. Because he feels a sense of wonder at the natural world, he is portrayed as an ignorant, but touchingly sensitive brute. But have you seen the trick? Because he is a caveman, we assume that he must be far inferior to us and that therefore his conclusion that there is a God who caused the thunder must, too, be inferior, primitive, and wrong.

But first, we don't know if the caveman actually did this sort of thing. And cavemen might not have been as educated as we are, but were they really so much more stupid? Are we sure cavemen wore crude skin clothes, grunted, and dragged their women around by their hair? We don't have any evidence of this. Some of the evidence we *do* have of the caveman's way of life, such as those sophisticated and beautiful paintings of animals in caves in Spain and France, suggests that whoever painted those graceful bison and deer were not primitive brutes.

If those cave artists observed the natural world with such sensitivity, they must also have gazed at the stars with awesome wonder, and perhaps they were frightened by the thunder. But in this were they really so very different from us? Which of us hasn't tried to create a work of art or been filled with wonder on a starlit night or frightened by a terrible storm?

If the caveman felt awe and wonder in the face of nature's power, is that really a sign of stupidity? Isn't it rather a sign of their heartfelt humanity? Neither does the feeling of awe rule out a greater understanding of something. It is perfectly possible to understand something and still feel awed by it. In principle, the caveman is really just the same as a mother who marvels at the beauty of her newborn baby, or a biologist who studies the intricate parts of nature and is amazed by the beautiful patterns he finds there. We may understand an event and still be struck dumb with wonder.

The Caveman's Conclusion

In other words, the caveman is being quite sensible, in his own way, to observe nature and see the signs of an unseen intelligence. Like most easy theories, this theory of where our religious instinct comes from is both right and wrong. It is right because it tells us that even primitive people can see the power of nature and conclude that there is a mind behind it all. However, the theory is wrong in what it assumes. It assumes that because we modern humans are not quite so frightened of thunder, and have telescopes to study the stars, we can conclude that there is no God.

The other thing the caveman got right was his idea that whoever was "out there" was stronger than he was. He may have concluded that this Great Spirit in the sky was angry with him and needed to be kept happy, but what is so very wrong with that conclusion?

As a basic starting point for religion, it sounds like common sense, doesn't it? If the caveman then started to think about his discovery and come to the idea that this Being was probably not all bad and fearsome, that, too, makes sense. Humans are always exploring their discoveries and learning more about them.

The question of how the human religious instinct developed is fascinating, but for now let's assume that the caveman was right.

In the forces of nature he sensed a larger force. He instinctively sensed that the forces of nature had to have some ultimate cause. The caveman may not have thought it all through logically, but like a child, he sensed this force, and he responded with fascination and curiosity. He wanted to know more.

This curiosity lies at the root of our own religious instinct, too. No matter who we are, we sense that there is more to life than meets the eye. Like the caveman, we see the beauty of the natural world; we marvel at the stars and the rolling thunder. But we also sense that the force behind them is active in our own lives. This unknown force exerts a powerful magnetic influence on us. We want to learn more about this mysterious presence, and that is what the religious quest is all about.

HOLD ON A MINUTE

What about the evils of religion?
I've started with the very basic question of whether there is a God or not, and maybe you don't have any arguments with what I've said so far. But then again, maybe you do. In fact, maybe you have some pretty tough and demanding questions you want to ask.

When I said that religion has been the source for some of the greatest achievements of the human race, you have thought, "But religion is also the source for the worst things in history! What about terrorism, witch hunts, the Spanish Inquisition, the troubles in Northern Ireland and in Israel? Think of all the torture, wars, and murder in the name of religion!"

It's true that terrible things have happened because of religious zeal (although probably not as terrible, or as many, as some people think). Some people have abused religion for their own ends, but we can't dismiss all religion because of that, any more than we should close down all the football stadiums because there are such things as football fanatics and ticket scalpers. There might be some crooked football fans, but it is impossible that everyone who likes football is mad or bad. Likewise, if virtually the entire human race has a religious instinct, there must be something to it, even if there are some religious people who are evil or crazy.

The universal religious instinct should make us ask if there really is a God out there or not. However, as soon as you say that there is a God, you are immediately faced with several more difficult questions.

The Big One

Anyone who believes in God will have to face the Big One — the most difficult problem of all. It is the question about suffering. You know how it goes: "If there is an all-loving, all-powerful God, why does he allow such terrible suffering in the world?" This is the best question anybody can ask about the existence of God.

Everyone is right to ask how we can possibly believe in a God who allows the horrors of concentration camps, terrorism, war, starvation, and natural disasters. I hope you don't mind if I put that question to the side for now. It's not that it can't be answered. Rather, the question is so important that I have to devote quite a bit of space to it in the next section.

The other reason I'd like to put that question to the side is that there are other problems that must be considered just to make sure the foundation for an answer is laid properly. The question about suffering and an all-loving God is jumping the gun, because we've only begun to consider the probability that some sort of God is out there. We haven't decided what that God is like. In other words, we haven't gotten to the point of saying that God is all-powerful and all-loving. We're still discussing whether he exists at all.

The Security-Blanket God

It's possible to acknowledge the universal religious instinct in humanity, but still not draw the conclusion that God must exist. You might say, "This universal religious instinct is just a feeling. No more and no less. Evolution has ingrained in us the desire to survive. However, we know death is around the corner, so the natural instinct is to deny death and hope that somehow we might go on living. Like the child who clings to his security blanket, we clutch the hope that there is a great and good Being out there who will keep us alive after death."

On the surface, this sounds plausible. It's easy to draw that conclusion because Christianity *does* worship a God who offers eternal life. However, that's not actually the way religion started. Most of the primitives' gods were fearsome beings who didn't promise eternal life. In fact, they didn't promise anything to anybody. Instead of offering life, they demanded death.

Part of some primitive religions was the offering of human sacrifices to keep the terrible gods happy. There was no idea of eternal life. The only thing you could hope for was that if your god was satisfied, he would make sure your harvest was good and he would protect you from the enemy tribe.

The idea of individual people enjoying life after death is a fairly recent development. The history of religion shows us that people worshiped their gods before they had the idea of an afterlife. Therefore, the idea that the religious instinct is simply the result of our wish to live forever can't be true.

Isn't Religion Just Wishful Thinking?

"Nevertheless," you might say, "the whole religious enterprise is just a form of wishful thinking. Because this life is hard, people imagine that a good God in heaven will make them happy."

Christianity Pure and Simple

It is true that some people worship a God who is like a big vending machine. They put prayer and worship in, and they expect God to make whatever they want come out. But I think this is a superstitious and immature form of religion. *Real* religion doesn't just dish out shallow happiness. Rather than fulfilling our wishes, real religion challenges our wishes. This is true of all religions. They make the most strenuous demands on people. All the great religions enforce strict moral codes. Jesus Christ says, "You cannot be my disciple unless you take up your cross and follow me."[1] In other words, authentic religion doesn't offer an easy life. Just the reverse: it offers a life that is more demanding than anything you can imagine.

Is God just a big, happy grandfather in the sky who religious people vainly hope will make them happy one day? It is true that we hope for final happiness. It is also true that we believe God loves us. But God's love is not sweet and fluffy like cotton candy. Instead, it is solid, severe, and awesome. Remember, those who believe in God also believe that God is their judge. If God is their judge, he holds them accountable for what they do with their lives. This is not exactly a cozy idea. If I were thinking wishfully, this is not the kind of God I would have invented.

Something Has to Keep Society Together

Other people argue that religion came about not because of wishful thinking, but because society needed it. "As people began to live in communities," they explain, "they needed certain taboos, such as 'You must not sleep with your brother's wife' or 'You must not kill pregnant cows.' Before long they saw that religion could help enforce these necessary taboos. The Great Being in the sky

[1] Cf. Luke 14:27.

was invoked as an ultimate source of punishment. If you broke the taboos, you not only endangered the tribe, but you might also be punished by God." For people with this opinion, religion is simply part of a necessary social structure. Over time it became complex and ornate, and full of doctrines and rules.

It is true that religion helps to support our families and our communities. But can that be the only source of our religious instinct? I don't think so, for two reasons. First, religion was there before the social taboos were. The first religious instinct had nothing to do with rules, and the first religions were simply rituals to keep the unpredictable gods happy. Because religion came before rules, the rules cannot be the root source for religion.

Second, while religion supports society, it also criticizes it. The priest, pastor, or prophet may work with the ruling power, but history shows us that in virtually every society, religious leaders have at times also felt obliged to contradict worldly rulers and point out where society is going wrong. The martyrs of every religion have been willing to die in their opposition to the society they were in.

And so, because religion came before rules, and because religion often finds itself at odds with society, we have to conclude that religion must be both older and bigger than society.

What You See Is What You Get?

Finally, there are some very practical-minded people who object to God and religion because it is all too complicated. "Look," they say, "all this complicated religious stuff is just hogwash. The world simply *is*. What you see is what you get. There is no God up there. What you think is a marvelous pattern in the world has been projected there by your own mind. That's it. End of story."

It's true that we don't actually *want* things to be so complex. We wish the world were simpler to understand. In fact, we often think things are rather easily explained, and then whenever we try to *really* understand something, we discover that it is more complicated than we could have imagined.

Indeed, the further and closer we look at the natural world, the more total understanding seems to slip away from us. We just about come up with a scientific theory and some detail arises that doesn't quite fit, and we are back to the drawing board. Experience shows us that reality is constantly more slippery and complicated than we had hoped. Wouldn't you suspect that if we were imagining a pattern, things would be a bit tidier?

Nevertheless, this sort of person insists that the complex pattern we see is simply the result of our minds' imposing some kind of order on everything. "In fact," they insist, "the universe is random and meaningless." Hold on. There's a hole in their bucket. Have you seen it?

If it is true that there is no pattern, and that everything is random, how would it be possible for someone to say so, since to think and speak you have to use a language with grammar?

Look at it this way: the whole process of thinking and speaking is logical. It is patterned, planned, and complex. If there is no plan or pattern in the universe, how could such a thing as human thought and language even come about? Could we think logically in a universe that is illogical? If everything were random, we would only be able to grunt at each other and wave our arms like madmen. So as soon as you say, "The universe has no meaning or pattern," you have proved yourself wrong, because you have thought and said something with meaning and pattern.

Finally, as I said, this way of thinking is like a leaky bucket. The leak is rather large, because, when you think about it, everything in the world may leak out the same hole. What I mean is: if there is no meaning or pattern, if everything is just in our mind, then the whole world, including ourselves, may also be no more than a random figment of our imagination. Is it really common sense to say that everything is just a dream inside our heads?

The Master Builder

There are only two choices: that the whole universe is meaningless and random, or that it is planned and meaningful. If it is random and meaningless, it is pretty hard to account for the evidence all around us.

We should ask ourselves which takes more faith: to believe that this complex, beautiful, and intricate universe happened purely by random chance, or to believe that there is a designer behind the whole thing. Like the caveman gazing at the stars, most people would draw the commonsense conclusion that since there is so much evidence that the world was designed, that there must be a designer.

The beauty and complexity of the world doesn't give us watertight proof for the existence of God, but it does give us plenty of evidence to infer it — on the basis of our common sense and the universal experience of the human race. However, accepting a designer for the universe is not the same thing as accepting the Christian God.

The first step is simply to accept that the religious instinct in human beings is on to something. That "Something" is bigger than all our wishes, dreams, and needs. It is greater than all the needs we have as either individuals or communities. That Something is the First Thing, the Thing from which everything else has come. If we have gotten that far, and are really convinced, then the next thing we need to ask is whether that Some*thing* is a Some*one*. If this force of creation and power exists, is it simply a vague energy source, or does it have a personality?

Christianity Pure and Simple

CAN THE FORCE BE WITH YOU?

The Energy Source for Life

In the film *Star Wars*, the wise old man Obi-Wan Kenobi introduces Luke Skywalker to "the Force." He explains to the young hero that the Force is the power behind the created universe, and that you can either fight for the good side of the Force, or be seduced by the dark side. The *Star Wars* films have been a tremendous success, not only because of the great storytelling and special effects, but also because they weave in another aspect of this universal religious feeling: that there is a battle between good and evil in the universe and that there is a guiding Force behind it all.

Most humans who admit the existence of God fall into two camps: those who believe God is a Someone, and those who believe God is Something. The latter, those who say God is an impersonal "Force," see behind all created things the "awful shadow of some unseen power." This power, however, remains vague, because it is far beyond anything we can imagine. All religions agree that God is greater than anything our minds can conceive. All agree that God is the energy source for all life. But some religions prefer to leave it there. The followers of Hinduism, Buddhism, New Age religions, and primitive religions hold to this view. If you like, they think God is a vast form of focused energy.

"The Force" is an excellent name for this God-power because you can think of it like electricity. This force or energy drives all things and holds all things together, but in the end it is an impersonal force. Like electricity, it doesn't have a mind or a will.

Beyond Good and Evil

A "Life Force" *does* seem to surge through all creation, and if God is simply the Life Force, it would explain why all the different religions seem to be headed in the same basic direction; for Christians, Jews, and Muslims also believe that God is the source and energy-force of creation. This idea of God, then, seems like a simple one that would solve all our problems and differences.

But if God is *only* the Life Force, this in fact raises more problems than it solves.

First, if God is merely the Life Force, then that force (because it has no personality) must be indifferent to what we call good and evil.

This is easy enough to understand if you think of the Life Force as electricity. Can electricity be good or evil? It seems good when it lights your desk, but it seems evil when it electrocutes your grandma. In fact electricity itself is neither good nor evil. In the same way, if what we call God is just the Life Force, then it is neither good nor evil. It can't decide anything one way or another.

If this Life Force is impersonal and has nothing to do with good and evil, then our concepts of "good" and "evil" must be an illusion. Some people take this line and say that a particular thing is only good or evil depending on your point of view. Good is what helps you to survive. Evil is what hurts you.

But are good and evil only useful illusions? The innate human sense of right and wrong is about more than just what happens to be pleasant for us or helps us survive. For example, what we consider to be good is often not pleasant. Being good is hard work. I would rather sit home and watch TV than go and visit my irritable, but lonely neighbor, or learn to play the piano.

Furthermore, what we consider most good often doesn't help us to survive at all. It does the opposite. If I die for my country or become disabled because I rescued a drowning child, everyone will think it good, even though, for me as an individual, it is not good at all. Good and evil, then, are actually bigger than what happens to be pleasant or helpful to us. Because of this, people have concluded that there is some ultimate source of good and evil that is above and beyond our own individual needs and desires.

Does the Force Have a Face?

For good and evil to exist, there has to be such a thing as choice. In other words, an action can be good or evil only if we have chosen it. If we had no choice in our lives, if we simply did what we are programmed to do by our genetic history or by our upbringing, then there could be no such thing as good and evil. We'd be simply acting out a destiny that had already been determined for us.

But as humans we all have a mind and a free will. We can "go with the Force" or "turn to the dark side." Where did this power to choose come from?

If the Life Force were just energy and not a person, it could not be the source for beings like us, who have minds and free will. Could the Life Force be inferior to the things it created? Could an energy force without a mind and will create beings with minds and wills? If so, how would the Life Force have thought of such beings in the first place?

However, if the Life Force also has a mind and a will, then in some sense it has personality. Therefore, Jews, Christians, and Muslims conclude that God is more than just the Life Force. We say that God is *personal*. In other words, the Force has a Face.

Is God Good?

As soon as we say, "God is personal" we don't mean that God is just a great big fellow who happens to live in the sky beyond space and time. What we mean is, instead of saying he is the "Force" of creation, we say he has an individual mind and will; that he is the

Mind and Will by whom all things were created, and by whom all things live and move and have their being.

Since he's not just a force, God can be good or evil. And Christians believe he is all-good.

But can God truly be all-powerful and all-good? Now we have come to that most troublesome question. If this personal God we've discovered is all-powerful and all-good, why does He allow evil? If he were all-good, he would want to stop evil from happening, and if he were all-powerful, he would be able to do what he wants. It is easy to conclude therefore, that if there is a God, he can't be all-good and all-powerful.

Good God/Bad God?

There are some religious systems that get around this problem by proposing that there are two equal and opposing gods or forces: a good force and a bad force. This is called *dualism*. Another form of dualism teaches that God holds within himself both the good and the evil, and that evil is simply the "shadow side" of God. There seems to be some common sense in this idea, since we know that in the world around us there is both good and evil.

But this view doesn't really hold up, because we also know that good and evil aren't equal forces. We know from experience that goodness is positive, original, and creative. Evil, on the other hand, is negative and parasitic. It isn't equal to good; it feeds on good. So a lie, for example, is nothing positive in itself; it is the absence of truth, or it is the truth twisted. Evil is an absence, not a presence. It is nothing new, but something broken that once was whole.

This is why Christians say there cannot be two equal gods — a bad one and a good one. Nor could God have any of that parasitic negative force within himself, for that which is all-positive and everlastingly creative must be utterly incompatible with anything that can only mock, twist, and destroy.

But back to the important question at hand. If God is truly all-good and all-powerful, how could he possibly allow evil?

Freedom to Turn to the Dark Side

The answer to the riddle is actually built into the question. When we say God is all-good and all-powerful, we are automatically saying that his goodness and power are very different from ours. In other words, because he can see and know everything, his goodness and power must be of a different order than what we're used to.

This means if God creates something, he cannot help but create it perfectly. Because God is all-good and all-powerful, he created everything, including human beings, as perfect as they could be. Part of that perfection is that he gave us a mind and a will. This is what the old creation story means when it says humans were created in God's image.

Having a mind means we can make decisions, and having free will means that we have the power to act on those decisions. If we have free will, we have the choice to do good or to do evil. Indeed, as I tried to show earlier, good and evil don't actually have any meaning *unless* we have the free will to choose. If you like, as soon as free will existed, so did good and evil.

If we didn't have this free will, we wouldn't have been created perfect. Would we have been more perfect if we were robots? I doubt it. However, you can see where this leads: if we have free will, there is the very real risk — in fact the very real probability — that sooner or later we will use that free will to choose evil. For if God forced us to do the right thing, it wouldn't be the right thing, because we wouldn't have chosen it freely.

Having created us with free will, God continues to extend that gift to us today. It's up to us. Will we choose good or choose evil? Because he is all-good, God will not force us one way or the other. We must conclude that for God to take away the gift of free will in order to stop suffering and evil would be an even worse evil. An all-good God who allows evil actions that inevitably lead to suffering is better than a God who would turn us into his robots.

The Downward Spiral

Now, there are other forms of suffering that are not caused by the bad choices of human beings. Natural disasters, for example, cause much human suffering. However, despite the terrible suffering they cause, natural disasters are not evil in themselves. They are merely part of the natural order. We suffer from them not because they are evil or because we have made a bad choice, but simply because we are in the wrong place at the wrong time.

Likewise, disease, birth defects, and accidents also cause terrible suffering in the world and cannot always be blamed on the bad choices of individual humans.

This kind of suffering, seemingly random and without blame, is part of a deeper problem. The violence of the natural world shows us that there is a fault line running right through the whole of the created order. Things aren't quite right. Violence, pain, and fear seem to be woven into the world at a deep level.

Psychologists even tell us that some of our illnesses and even many of our accidents are caused by stress, anger, aggression, and violence. The world is more complicated than we imagine, and the causes of all events are interrelated. It may be that in some dark pattern, even the natural disasters, birth defects, and accidents are part of the negative effects of the bad choices of the whole human race.

That doesn't mean we are all to blame for our own suffering. Often we are the victims of the bad choice of another person. We live in a world that is riddled with hidden horrors — shot through with bad choices and the twisted results of those bad choices. The beauty of the world is darkened by evil, and we're right to question God about this grim fact.

The Price of Freedom

God has an answer, but just as the question isn't an easy one, so the answer isn't easy. If all the evil in some mysterious way comes back to the bad choices of the human race, we have to conclude that God must have foreseen all the suffering that would result from our bad choices, and considered it worth the risk.

But it may not be quite as grim as it sounds. It may be, too, that the suffering, in the long run, teaches us lessons that we could not learn in any other way. Maybe, in some mysterious and terrible way, we are becoming more perfect by going through the evil and coming out on the other side than if we had never gone through it at all — just as a muscle becomes stronger through being strained, exerted, and torn, then rebuilt.

I said the question of suffering was vitally important. It is important because it brings us to the very heart of God and to the very heart of the Christian faith. Some people think Christianity is simply a happy-clappy religion that skirts the enormous problem of suffering. Nothing could be further from the truth. As we shall see throughout this book, struggling with the problem of human suffering is precisely what Christianity is all about.

Rather than giving an intellectual answer to the problem, the Christian religion is itself the solution to the problem. The answer to the problem of suffering runs through the whole story of Christianity like a scarlet thread in a vast and beautiful tapestry.

Is Anybody There?

If you really want to answer the question of suffering, you can't be satisfied with mere intellectual answers. Each one of us is stuck in the middle of the problem of suffering, because we all suffer. Finding the answer requires getting involved and struggling to work out the problem — not just with our heads, but with our hearts and our whole lives.

This is far from easy, because one of the symptoms and causes of the suffering is the fact that we are confused and cut off from the answer. We are cut off from God. Like wounded, lost children, we are in pain and we do not know where to turn. The next thing we have to consider is how God might be trying to wade into our confused, lost state to find us and bring us home.

HIDE AND SEEK

Our Choices Guide Our Destiny

At the heart of every great story is some great conflict. A clever author weaves the hero's individual problems into the greater struggle between good and evil that drives the plot forward. This is nowhere more true than in the great stories in the Bible. From the beginning we not only see humanity asking theoretical questions about good and evil, but we see human beings locked into a battle of choices and actions that have everlasting consequences.

The ancient story of the Garden of Eden shows us the situation. God created men and women with free will, but without the knowledge of good and evil. He placed them in a beautiful primeval paradise and gave them one commandment: they should not taste the fruit from the tree of the knowledge of good and evil.

As the story goes, they used their will to make a bad choice: they disobeyed God's command and ate of the tree. As soon as they had chosen badly, they *did* have the knowledge of good and evil, and part of that knowledge was that they felt guilty. Their first instinct was to run and hide from God. Suddenly, instead of being content in God's presence, they began to fear God and do anything they could to stay away from him.

God, however, was not going to let them go. He came to find them and asked them what had gone wrong. When they told him, he had to expel them from the Garden of Eden, to wander the earth as exiles. Worst of all, they would have to grow old and die; otherwise they would live in their twisted condition forever.

The ancient religious stories are full of simple wisdom. They can be far richer than intellectual arguments about the existence of God, and about the nature of good and evil. The Garden of Eden story outlines the stark truth about our human condition quite simply. Men and women choose to disobey God's plan for their lives. This makes them suspicious of each other, unsure of themselves, and fearful of God.

As a result, their instinct is to hide from God. Adam and Eve's expulsion from paradise symbolizes the fact that we all wander in a hard and dangerous land, full of anger, violence, and fear. This is the spiritual condition of the human race. We live in a land of exile, where we are cut off from God, cut off from eternal life, and cut off from real happiness.

Here I Come, Ready or Not

The Garden of Eden story also shows us what God is like. He doesn't wash his hands of Adam and Eve. Although they are hiding, he comes to find them. Even though he expels them from paradise, the later chapters of the book of Genesis show that God stays with them.

In other words, God does not forsake what he has made. He is always on a search-and-rescue mission. Like a salvage expert, he goes out and about, seeing what can be hauled up, recycled, rescued, and restored. He doesn't want us to be lost forever. He wants to straighten out the twist in our character and put us on the road back to Eden.

But God has a problem: we are very good at hiding. Ever since Eden we have learned to run and hide not only in the bushes, but within any bit of cover we can find. Furthermore, part of this inherited twist in our nature is the habit of blaming God for doing the hiding. We realize he is difficult to follow and understand, so we say that it's *his* fault and that he is distant and unconcerned about us.

Wake Up

Many religions speak of the beginning of the religious quest as "waking up." It is as if, in our natural human state, we are dozing. We are spiritually asleep and need a wake-up call. It is easy to stay in bed, and difficult to open our eyes to the light.

But if we are to make any progress in our knowledge of God, we must first ask God to wake us up. We have to open our eyes and see that God has been there all the time, waiting for us to wake up. In fact, rather than being distant, he has been closer to us than we are to ourselves. Instead of hiding, he has constantly been trying to reveal himself to us.

If God wants us to be aware of his presence and to learn more about him, how would he make himself known? God speaks to us in four general ways, which interact with each other, working together to help us see God and understand how we can get back to the garden of perfection. Seeing God with our minds is only one aspect of the plan. He also wants us to be involved with our hearts, our wills, and our bodies, to understand who he is and what we should do, and then to do something about it.

In other words, it is not enough for us to open our eyes and wake up. We also have to get up, get dressed, get washed, and get a life.

If I Only Had a Brain

In the first part of this chapter, I said the arguments for the existence of God take us only so far. Our intellectual processes can help us to figure out that God exists. They can also help us deduce what God is like. However, those intellectual processes are not foolproof. If you are clever enough, and have the desire, you can use statistics, science, logic, and argument to prove or disprove almost anything. If only we had brains that were totally reliable! As it is, they are leaky buckets. What we know with our brains we only know in part.

This is because our brains were never intended to be just logical computing machines. We were never meant to be pure intellect. Our brains work together with our bodies. Brains do not just process ideas and form conclusions. They also register all the stimuli from our senses and form all those sensations into a picture of the physical world around us.

Furthermore, our brains help us to find meaning in the world that our senses perceive. Our brain evaluates and decides what is good and evil and which option we should take. Finally, our brains are used in the powerful experience of love. Through relationships with others — through talking, laughing, arguing, crying, making love, making war, and making up, we come to the fullest understanding of life.

Four Ways to Find God

Our brains and bodies work together in four ways to help us discover God. These ways are not purely logical. Instead they involve our heads, our hearts, and our bodies. First, we are able to observe the world and make reasonable conclusions about it; secondly, we are able to perceive beauty; thirdly, we can discern right and wrong; and fourthly, we can experience something called *love*. I've spent most of this first part of the book trying to engage that first, intellectual ability to know God, but that's only part of the story.

The first way to find God is to look around you. The world is God's creation, and it tells us what God is like in the same way that a poem, a play, or a painting reveals the personality of the writer or artist. By observing nature we can gather that God has created an ordered and complex world, both beautiful and terrible.

But we can also gather that something has gone wrong with his creation. Humans aren't the only ones who are troubled by fear, violence, and death. Nature may be beautiful, but it is also cruel. Nature itself seems somehow cut off and alienated from total harmony. Things go wrong. The earth quakes, and mountains explode. Violent storms destroy life. Sometimes it seems that all creation writhes in torment, and the turmoil tells us that there is not only harmony, but discord in God's world.

If this is so, then God's world is a place of conflict, struggle, and striving. There is a battle going on, and our participation in that battle will help us to understand more about God himself.

Beauty Is Truth and Truth Beauty

We recognize the battle that is going on, but within the battle we often respond with feelings of desire, longing, and awe. In other words, we feel that the world is beautiful. We also have a deep sense that what is beautiful is also true, and what is true always has an air of beauty about it. We often decide what is true and beautiful by relating it back to nature. The more natural a thing is, the more we consider it to be true and beautiful. So, although we might like silk flowers, real roses will win every time. That is because real roses are both truer and more beautiful than silk roses.

Our sense of beauty, then, points us to truth, and this unlocks another secret of God's personality. The world he has created has an inner logic, simplicity, and unity that we look to as a model for all that is beautiful and true.

We might disagree about the relative beauty in the world around us. You might like beaches while I love rugged mountains. Furthermore, there is a whole second level of beauty and truth created when human beings make things. Yet each form of beauty and truth, from music and drama to poetry and paintings, points us to a beauty and truth beyond and above this earthly plane. The beauty and truth we see around us are not infallible pointers to God, but they do reveal more of what God is like. So we conclude that God is the source of beauty and truth, and thus, he must have that simplicity, unity, and beauty to an overwhelming degree.

The Good, the Bad, and the Ugly

The sense of beauty and truth helps us to discern what God is like, but along with this instinct for beauty and truth we also have a sense of right and wrong. People might not agree on the details, but they all agree that there is such a thing as right behavior and wrong behavior. For example, some people might think it is all right to have ten wives. Others think you may have only one. But almost all agree that you mustn't sleep with another man's wife.

Our moral instinct is another pointer to God's personality. Since we all have this general sense of right and wrong, God must be the ultimate source of what is right. However, this is the sense that needs the most instruction.

Just as what is beautiful and true is usually that which is most natural, you might think that what is "right" is what is also that which is "natural." But what seems natural to some people is most certainly not right. So, for example, some people think it is the most natural thing in the world to steal or lie or cheat to further their own ends. Such people have forgotten what is truly natural, confusing it with whatever feels right at the moment. They have slipped into a distorted mind-set in which they consider unnatural actions and desires to be natural and good.

This kink in our character is what needs correction, and that is why we believe God revealed through the Jewish religion a code of right behavior. This was not to make everyone feel guilty, but to tell us what we *ought* to be like. It reminds us that we were created in God's image, and to be truly natural we ought to be very different from what we sometimes are.

Furthermore, once we get a glimpse of what we ought to be like, we also get a glimpse of what God is like. In other words, when we see how totally natural and good we are meant to be, we can see that God is totally natural and therefore totally good. He is as he should be. He lives in a simple condition in which all that he is and does is good.

God Is Love

If God is beautiful, true, and good, then part of that goodness means he is active and outgoing. Goodness is, by its nature, creative and positive. Goodness does not stay bottled up, but reaches out to those around it. Therefore God must be actively involved in promoting goodness, truth, and beauty in the world.

The Bible affirms this by telling us that God is love. In other words, at the very core of God's being is this mysterious power we call *love*. This is not a sentimental kind of love. This is not a sweet emotion. Instead it is a powerful, overwhelming desire for the good of others. It is a passion for the perfection of beauty and truth and goodness. It is an ever-increasing spiral of outgoing dynamic power that wishes to reach out and reconcile all things in its embrace. In other words, God is in a loving relationship with the universe and everything in it.

This love is not only what God does. It is what he *is*. God is not only in a relationship; he *is* relationship. This is one of the reasons Christians have understood God to be a *Trinity:* Three Persons in One. In a magnificently mysterious way we believe that at the core of God is a loving relationship between Father, Son, and Holy Spirit.

Logic is useful, but it is *love* that really helps us find our way to God. Learning about God does not mean simply studying books of theology; it means entering into a relationship with him. To learn about God we do not just study beauty, truth, and goodness. We enter into Beauty, Truth, and Goodness. The Old Testament talks about "knowing" God, and the word *knowing* is the same word it uses to describe the intimate relationship between husband and wife.

It is through the drama of human love, with all its hopes and fears, all its triumphs and tragedies, that we really find God. It is not in formal religion and intellectual theories alone, but also in the stories of real people, and their struggles with good and evil, joy and sorrow, that we discover God. And while we search for God in this same human story, we discover that all the time he has been searching for us.

KNOWING GOD

Knowledge Comes from Experience
Anyone who has learned to ride a bike knows that we learn better by doing than by being told. We learn to ride a bike by

hopping on and pedaling — and falling down and doing it again. It would be easier just to read a book about how to ride a bike, but actually trying to ride one is far more effective. It is also far more dangerous. Reading about bikes involves no risks. Riding a bike means crashes and grazed knees.

Knowing God is just the same. Although study comes into it, we're talking about an activity, not a spectator sport. Knowing about God and knowing God are not the same thing. Knowing God is far more like making friends with a person than learning facts about that person. It is in doing things with a person that we learn most about him, and so it is in living life with God that he reveals himself to us most powerfully. God reveals himself to us through our own relationship with him, but he also reveals himself as we learn about his relationship with other people.

Show Me, Don't Tell Me

If God is love, and if he is best known within a relationship, you would expect religion to be concerned with stories about God's relationship with people. In fact, most religions do just that. They tell stories about God's interaction with human beings.

These religious stories show us what God is like because they show what he *does*. Stories are truth in action. They reveal God's personality and unlock the way he deals with people.

However, the religious stories of the world are not all straightforward. Some are myths and legends — stories about gods, goddesses, and human beings that no one pretends are actual real, historical figures. These stories are useful, because they reveal the truths of that particular religion. The stories "incarnate" the religious principles and ideas. The word *incarnate* simply means "to put flesh on." The stories of the various religions flesh out the teachings about God.

The Myth of the Hero

The stories from many religions around the world vary enormously, but there is one type of story that comes up time and time again. The story of the hero's quest arises in almost every culture and at every time down through history, from ancient India to the latest Hollywood film.

The story of the hero's quest is simple. The hero is a special person who must leave his home to set out on a great adventure. Usually he has to find some treasure or rescue a loved one. But the outer quest also has an inner meaning. The hero may be looking for a Golden Fleece or a magic sword, but he is also looking for spiritual enlightenment, salvation, and eternal life. To do this he has to overcome great difficulties, defeat a terrible enemy, and gain the prize.

The hero's story shows us how to fight life's battles, but it also shows us that we are all on a spiritual quest to find God. The ultimate prize is not just happiness, health, and wealth, but spiritual enlightenment, salvation, and eternal life.

In most religions, the various kinds of myths have no link with history. The stories help people on their own spiritual quest, but everyone knows the hero is not a real person; or if he was real, that the story has been made much more elaborate to teach the necessary lessons. Hero stories crop up in every religion and culture, but there is one religious tradition that is startlingly different. In the Jewish religion, the heroes are all portrayed as real people. They are not magical figures from wonderful fairytales. Instead they are presented as historical characters who lived in a real relationship with God himself.

As a result, when you read the book of Genesis you find that Abraham traces his ancestry back to Noah, and from Noah to Adam. In other words, the Hebrew writers are keen to show that

Abraham was a descendant of that first person with whom God had established a special relationship. If Adam was created in God's image as a son of God, then Abraham, as Adam's descendant, is also part of the same family. This is a curious detail, and one that becomes very important later on in the story.

The Saga of God's Family

The Old Testament is a bit like one of those soap operas about the life and loves of a vast extended family. It is in fact a saga of one family's unique relationship with God. The father of the family was Abraham. He was the chieftain of a nomadic tribe in the Middle East sometime around 2000 BC. He lived with the great civilizations of Babylon to the East and Egypt to the southwest, and wandered in the territory that is now the nation of Israel and Palestine. In the book of Genesis God promises Abraham a large family and a rich land, if he would only step out and follow God's lead.

The problem was, Abraham was childless. But late in their lives, Abraham's wife Sarah bears a son called Isaac. In a very strange and terrible story, God asks Abraham to sacrifice his son Isaac on a hill called Moriah. As they are going up the mountain the boy asks his father why he has no animal for the sacrifice. Abraham says to his son, "God himself will provide the sacrifice."[2] Then, at the last minute, God calls from heaven that Abraham should kill a ram instead, and the boy's life is spared.

Hints and Guesses

I took a moment to relate that disturbing story from the book of Genesis because it illustrates another curious fact about the Jewish

---

[2] Cf. Gen. 22:8.

people. All through the Old Testament we get the impression that they are living in the future. They are always looking forward with hope to the promises of God.

No matter how down-and-out they are, no matter how much they rebelled against God, still they eventually turn back to him. In a rather poignant way, the Jews were a hopeful people. No matter how desperate their situation, they always trusted that God would bring them into something better.

The story of Abraham nearly killing his son is one of those strange "pointers" forward. When Abraham says, "God himself will provide a sacrifice," he is getting a glimpse of the future. The story is littered with these hints and clues about a wonderful future, so that all through the Old Testament we get the picture that God is laying a plan. Through the complicated joys and sorrows of this one tribe we get the picture that God is working out his plan not only for them, but for the whole human race.

Slavery and Freedom

Throughout the stories of the Old Testament God reveals through the history of the Jewish people what we human beings are like, and what he is like. This is the marvelous way God speaks — not primarily through a law or through theological teachings, but through the drama of one family's roller-coaster ride through history.

As the story moves on, Abraham's great-grandson Joseph is sold by his brothers to be a slave in Egypt. Then, when a great famine hits the land, the brothers travel to Egypt to get food and are saved by the same Joseph, who has now become the Pharaoh's regent and governor of the whole country.

Joseph's brothers settle in Egypt, but several generations later their descendants — the Hebrew people — have become slaves.

However, they did not forget the promise of a great nation and a great land.

A fugitive from Egypt, a Hebrew called Moses, is summoned by God to go back to Egypt and lead the people to freedom. At that point God promises, "I will raise up from among the people a prophet like you."

Part of Moses' task is to give the people God's law and to set up a religious system for them to follow. Part of that religious system is a system of animal sacrifice. The other religions of the Middle East had animal (and human) sacrifice, but they sacrificed animals to please angry gods in order to have fair weather and good harvest. Moses sets up a system in which sacrifice wins forgiveness for breaking God's law. The theory was that your punishment for sin would be taken by the animal, and you would be forgiven.

Signs and Symbols

This sacrificial system is another one of God's hints, and the way he takes an existing religious idea and transforms it is typical of the Old Testament. Time and again God works through the religious genius of the Jews to take a crude way of thinking about God and remake it to reveal what he is *really* like. For pagan peoples the sacrificial animal was offered as meat for a hungry god to devour. But God wanted this religious action to carry a more profound and beautiful meaning.

When Moses leads the Hebrews from slavery in Egypt, God asks them to sacrifice a perfect lamb. This Passover Lamb (also called the Lamb of God) is killed so that their oldest sons would not die when God sends the angel of death to visit Egypt.

This sacrifice is not performed to please God, but to deliver the Hebrew children from death. The ceremony echoes the sacrifice that Abraham made to deliver *his* son from death. It also points forward to another Lamb of God, a final sacrifice that would one day deliver all of humanity from death. Eventually the Hebrew people do go into the land that is now Israel, and once they arrive there, God chooses a shepherd boy to be their king.

Prophets and Priests

In God's way of using signs, actions, and picture language, the shepherd boy David becomes the symbol of another Shepherd-King who would one day come to rule his people. In the whole history of the Jewish people, God gradually reveals himself. He doesn't simply tell them what he is like. Instead he is there with them, as a father is with his child, going beside them and teaching them by showing and doing rather than by telling.

In this way the truth of who God is and what he is like is being lived out within history. God reveals his character to them within their experience as a nation, as individual families, and as individual people. We can see that it is God's way to reveal himself within the very fabric of life.

The Jewish religious system was maintained by priests who were drawn from a special tribe of men. The priests conducted the religious rituals for the people. The priests also instructed the people in the religion and kept the whole system going, just as priests and clergy do today.

However, there was another breed of religious leaders who were not quite so humdrum and part of the establishment. The prophets were men who were inspired by God to preach to the people. They stirred the people up with dramatic actions, radical preaching, and an uncompromising message. The message was that God loved his people; he was unhappy that they continually turned away from his ways, and he called them time and again to return to friendship and fellowship with him.

Is Anybody There?

The Return of the King

King David lived around 1000 BC. His son Solomon would build up the dynasty of David to a point of great power and glory, but within five hundred years, the kingdom would fall and the people would be taken into exile. Nevertheless, the prophets tell them not to give up hope. God will bring them back to the land, and one day a new son of David will be their king.

God sends various prophets to look forward to the coming of the King in different ways. One says that God will be the Shepherd of his people, then says that the coming King will also be the Shepherd of his people. Another says that a virgin will give birth to a child who will be called Emmanuel, which means "God is with us."[3] The prophet Isaiah says that this promised one will be the "Servant of God"[4] and that he will end up suffering terribly to redeem the people. The prophet Daniel has a vision in which he sees "one like the Son of Man"[5] sitting at God's right hand. This "Son of Man" is one who appears like a human being, and yet has the glory and majesty and power of God.

For two thousand years, from the time of Abraham onward, God works in a unique way in the history of the Jews. They are a chosen race, not because they are superior somehow, but because they have a unique faith. This faith doesn't make them perfect; their history is one of spectacular failures and disastrous choices. But despite their failings, they are God's people, and through them he works out his plan for the whole human race. Through the Jews, God promises a new King — a chosen one — one anointed to bring in an everlasting kingdom of peace and justice for all. The

---

[3] Isaiah 7:14; Matthew 1:23.
[4] Cf. Isaiah 42:1.
[5] Daniel 7:13.

prophecies about this King are mysterious, but they are clear that he will be unique, and that he will come to perform a special function in the world.

By the time of the Roman Empire the Jews have returned to their land, and they are looking forward to the promised King. At this point in history God's revelation of himself comes to a climax. The time of hints and guesses, signs and symbols ends, and the ultimate revelation of God is about to burst upon human history.

Chapter Two

The God-Man

THE ULTIMATE REVELATION

Suppose you were God. You created men and women to be your sons and daughters. You wanted them to be part of your family; you wanted them to be happy. But they turned away from you. Because they turned away from you, their human nature became twisted. Suddenly their instinct was to hide from you.

They wanted to hide for two reasons. First, they assumed you were angry with them, and they were afraid. Second, something inside them whispered that it would be far more fun and interesting to do things their own way.

This is what Christians mean by *Original Sin*. When we say that a baby is born with Original Sin, we're not saying that the baby is terribly wicked. We are simply acknowledging that the baby, like every one of us, was born "twisted," and that this is a basic flaw in human character — like a bad note in a beautiful piece of music.

Likewise, when Christians say that every human being is a sinner, we are not saying that everyone is totally and utterly evil. Instead we are admitting that, although everyone is created in the image of God, this perfect image gets distorted by selfishness, violence, and greed. In other words, our goodness is stained, and we need a good scrub.

This is common sense, isn't it? When we look in the mirror, or when we look at other people, we see human beings who are basically good. However, in each of us there is also a shadow side. In some people the rottenness has spread and they have become more bad than good. But most of us mean well. At heart we desire what is good and true.

Original Sin does not mean that we are rotten to the core. It means at a very basic level we are cut off from God. Instead of running toward him, we are running away. Instead of looking for him, we are hiding from him. One of the results of our hiding from God is that we can't see him clearly. In fact, without his help, we can't see him at all. We're all in this fix together — the blind leading the blind.

So, What Would You Do?

Since we all have this flaw in our character, we have trouble seeing what is best for us. Despite receiving good advice from wise and holy people, we make wrong choices. The situation is similar to that of a family in which loving parents have to deal with a rebellious teenager. The parents know what is best, but their goodwill is met with sullen behavior. To their great sorrow, the parents watch their teenager constantly reject all that is best for him, leading to sometimes disastrous decisions.

This is why the stories in the first part of the Bible (the Old Testament), which tell of the relationship between the Jewish people and God, are so interesting — not because they give us a beautiful new religion or because the Jewish people are the perfect followers of a spiritual form of life. Instead, the stories capture our imagination because they are a catalog of human disasters. Time and again the Jewish people mess up. They reject God; they disregard his law and wind up as miserable failures.

The God-Man

Because their instinct was to fear God, the people of the Old Testament sometimes perceived God as being angry with his people. It is true that sometimes the Old Testament God comes across as angry and vengeful, but more often he is shown to be patient and forgiving. An ancient Jewish poet says God is "slow to anger and rich in mercy."[6] And through the voice of the Old Testament preachers, God cries out, "O my people, what have I done to you? What have I done to make you turn away from me?"[7]

God sees that we are like sheep without a shepherd. We long for happiness, and we are searching everywhere to find it. At the same time, God sees that we are running from the very source of happiness, which is he. But how can God get through to us if there is a part of us that instinctively runs and hides from him? How can God reveal himself to us, if our eyes are shut tight? What would you do if you were God?

Getting Through

First of all, God made sure that a hunger for goodness remained within each one of us. Because God made us, no matter who we are there will always be a part of us that searches for God. This is where the religious instinct in humans comes from. In fact, it is so strong that we are looking for God even when we think we are running away from him.

When we desire something beautiful, deep down we are searching for God, the source of beauty. Our desire for youth and our fear of death and old age is really our desire for eternal life, and that, too, is a desire for God. When we want what is good and true, or when we cry out for justice, we are expressing our desire for God.

[6] Cf. Psalm 103:8.
[7] Cf. Micah 6:3.

In all these ways, at the very depth of our being, we long for God. We can't help it. It is written into our nature.

However, our natural search for God can take us only so far. Remember, there is a flaw in our nature, so that while we long for God, we also turn away from him. In a similar way we want beauty, truth, goodness, and justice, but that which is totally beautiful, true, good, and just also seems severe and scary. We long for love, and yet we are frightened of being consumed by the very love we long for.

Making a Prophet

In the second part of the Old Testament, the Jewish writers begin to speak the language of love. The prophets were holy men who taught the Jewish people about God in a vivid and powerful way. In many ways the Jewish prophets tell us that God loves his people.

They say God is like a passionate lover who seeks and pursues the beloved everywhere. He is a faithful husband who loves his wife no matter what she does. The ancient Jewish writers tell us that God is a good and gentle shepherd. He is a wise and gracious king, a patient father, and a long-suffering servant. The prophets say he is a faithful God: although we might turn away from him, he will never turn away from us.

Out of all these images of love, one image came into focus. First and foremost God reveals that he is a loving *father*. In a way, then, his love is like human love. Yet it is so far greater that it is not like our human love at all. Our love is always mixed up with false motives, fantasy, and selfishness. But God's love is totally pure and real. It is never selfish. God does not love others because he wants to be loved himself. Instead he loves others simply for who they are. God's real love is unconditional. It is also active. It takes the initiative. It reaches out and draws the loved one into an everlasting embrace.

The Author Steps on Stage

Real love is also *sacrificial*. If you really love something or someone, you will even go through pain and suffering to win that love. All along we had thought God was the stern judge, a distant creator, or a vengeful tyrant; but instead God is like a vulnerable and faithful Father.

By giving us freedom to choose, God subjects himself to our will. In allowing us to run away from him, God allows himself to be rejected and despised. This is a shock. It upsets all our expectations and prejudices. No wonder it took two thousand years for such an astounding truth to sink in!

The message of the Old Testament prophets was that God's love for his people was so great that he would continue to reach out despite their continual rejection. To do this he planned to send a messenger who would communicate his love in a new and unforgettable way.

We can communicate with our loved ones with letters, cards, and gifts. But in the end we want to come and be with them. We want to speak to them face-to-face. This is what God chose to do. All the symbols and signs pointed to this end: God would come and visit his people.

The earlier Jewish writers said God was like a shepherd and a king, but the later writers said the Shepherd-King would appear. When the Jewish people escaped from slavery, they sacrificed an innocent lamb, but their later prophets said the sacrificial Lamb of God would come to them in a startling way.

They would no longer have to interpret vague prophecies and learn about God's love through religious writings. There would be no need to read about him in signs and symbols, because all the symbols were about to be shown clearly. There was no need to read a biography, because the subject of the book was about to enter the room. The time for stories and plays was over, because the author was about to step onto the stage.

MOTHER AND CHILD

God's Secret Plan

Throughout the history of the Jewish people, God was setting the stage. First of all, he was showing that he is not a distant deity, but a God who is involved with real people at real places in real time. The saga of the Jewish nation incarnated God; it fleshed out God's character so we could understand (by his actions) what he was really like.

But the Old Testament story, with its symbols and signs of promise, also pointed to a more powerful incarnation of God yet to come.

Adam had been created in the image of God, but that image became soiled when he chose his own way instead of God's way. One of the consequences of the bad choice was that, from then on, human beings would face suffering and death.

To rescue humans from this curse of suffering and death, and to restore the divine image in them, God himself planned to take human form and secretly enter the world to put things right. Where Adam the human had put things wrong, God himself (become human himself) would put them right.

Christians believe that God took human form the way all of us do: born as a baby of a human mother. But how could God take human form when all human beings carried in their nature that fatal flaw that we call Original Sin?

To solve the problem God intervened in a unique way when a little girl was conceived. When two ordinary people called Anna and Joachim made love, God made sure that the child who was conceived was free from the distortion of Original Sin. This baby girl was unique among all human beings, and she is known to us as Mary, the mother of Jesus.

Mary was kept free from Original Sin for two reasons. First, God's human form had to be as fresh and perfect as Adam's had been. Second, a free choice had to be made. God couldn't force himself on Mary. She could bear God's human form into the world only by saying yes to God. So that she could choose freely, her mind unclouded, Mary had to be kept free from Original Sin.

An Amazing Yes

Remember, one of the symptoms of Original Sin is that we instinctively choose the wrong way. The twist in our nature means we have a built-in tendency to say no to God. Because of this, we are not wholly free; we have a bias toward choosing wrongly. For Mary's choice to be really free, her will had to be free of this bias. This didn't mean she would automatically say yes to God. It simply meant that she had total freedom to choose without the built-in bias that comes with Original Sin.

Mary's perfection doesn't mean she was some kind of superwoman. In fact she was very ordinary. To understand this kind of perfection, we need to think of something that is perfectly natural, like a forest. When you are in the forest, you might notice that it is beautiful and whole. Everything is working as it should work. However, that perfection seems ordinary because it is natural, and what is natural is not unusual. We don't exclaim with surprise when the sun comes up or when water runs downhill. In that same natural and wholesome way, Mary was perfect. She didn't have the flaws and distortions of character that everyone else has. She was simply all that a human woman should be.

Because of the special natural perfection that God gave her, an angel of God recognized that Mary was "full of grace."[8] *Grace* is another word for the goodness of God, so we believe that this ordinary Jewish girl was full of God's goodness. Because she was full of God's goodness she could perfectly cooperate with God when he asked if she would be willing to conceive and bear his Son into the world.

This fullness of goodness did not take away Mary's free will and independence. God's grace did not mean Mary was God's robot — far from it. Instead this fullness of God's grace meant that Mary was fully human and fully free. She could have said no to God when he asked her to give everything, but at that crucial moment of freedom Mary said yes.

Son of God and Son of Man

Christians believe that Mary remained a virgin as she conceived and gave birth to Jesus. Jesus didn't have an earthly father. Instead, by a unique miracle, Mary became pregnant by the power of God.

When Mary said yes to God she became pregnant, and God took real human form in the little boy Mary named Jesus. The name *Jesus* was an ordinary Jewish name at that time, but the name also means "God saves." Christians believe that this Jesus was at once totally God and totally human: not some mixture of the two, not a God in human skin or merely a wise and powerful man. Because Jesus is God in human form, we say rightly that Mary is the "Mother of God."

[8] Luke 1:28.

Now, if you have been thinking this through at all, you should be saying, "Whoa! Are you expecting me to swallow this?!" You really think God took human form? You believe Mary became pregnant by God? That's mind-blowing!"

You're right. These claims for Jesus are incredible. The miracles surrounding Mary's life and Jesus' birth are not easy to believe. But stay with it. Remember, the people who lived in Jesus' time didn't find it easy to believe either, and yet certain events occurred to make them see that these conclusions were really the only possible ones.

Are Miracles Possible?

Most any sensible person would, of course, step back with disbelief at the idea that God took human form in Jesus Christ.

Did this incredible miracle really happen? To decide whether this is possible, we first have to ask whether we believe miracles are possible. If we conclude that miracles are possible, then we have to ask whether this *particular* miracle could have happened.

As to the first question, there are really only two choices. The first choice is that the universe we live in is closed; that it operates by set laws of nature that never change. If this is so, then everything can be understood by scientific observation. If the universe we live in is closed, then miracles simply cannot happen.

The other choice is that the universe is open-ended. In other words, although there are set laws of nature, the God of nature can suspend those laws if he has good reason.

Which choice is more likely to be the right one? If we believe there is a God who exists above and beyond nature, and who created the natural laws, then we have to conclude (at least in theory) that God can work beyond the limits of those laws, and therefore what we call *miracles* can happen.

Unnatural and Supernatural

Miracles may therefore be possible, but impossibilities are not possible. In other words, God may produce a miracle, but even he cannot do something contrary to reason. He cannot make a circle square. He cannot make two plus two equal seven. A miracle, therefore, is not something that goes against nature. It is a unique and unexpected action that happens within nature.

We may wonder, for instance, how Jesus turned water into wine, as the Bible reports. Yet in the natural cycle of things, water turns into wine all the time. Rainwater falls and is drawn up into vines that produce grapes that are pressed into wine. Jesus' miracle didn't change nature. It simply speeded things up. How did Jesus walk on water? Walking on water is not an eternal impossibility. We can all walk on water when it's frozen. Jesus didn't suspend or contradict nature; he simply shifted the way it normally works.

The same is true when we think about the miraculous conception of Mary without sin. This unique event does not go against the law of nature. It is not unnatural for a person to be sinless. Indeed, that is our perfectly natural condition. That's how we were first made. When God intervened to make sure Mary had no human flaw, he was not doing something unnatural, but was restoring what was most natural.

Likewise when Mary conceived Jesus without having made love to a man, God was not doing something totally unnatural or contrary to the laws of nature. Young women get pregnant. What *would* have been unnatural would be for Joseph to have gotten pregnant. So what happened to Mary was not unnatural. It was *supernatural*. In other words, a power greater than nature did something natural in a unique and unexpected way.

This is the kind of miracle we are talking about. Because he created the natural world, God has the power to intervene in that world. We believe that in order to further his plan for the world, God took a few unique actions within nature, over the course of history.

Science and Science Fiction

Despite my explanations, you wouldn't be a sensible person unless you still found it all too much to take. God comes down to earth and takes human form? An ordinary girl becomes pregnant with God's son? It sounds a little bit like a science-fiction story, doesn't it? Where did the Christians get such a far-fetched idea in the first place?

I said earlier that they came to these astounding conclusions because of the rest of Jesus' life.

Jesus came on the scene just like any other traveling Jewish preacher. In his time there were other preachers who healed people and gathered crowds around them. There were other religious leaders who had little bands of followers.

Indeed, throughout the world, both before and after Jesus, there have been many religious leaders who have spoken for God. In most cases their followers don't claim that they were God in human form. And yet, within a few years of his death, Jesus' disciples were teaching quite clearly that Jesus was indeed the Son of God, and that his mother was a virgin, and that he was born as the result of a miracle. Why did the disciples of Jesus come up with such astounding and incredible views?

They came to their conclusions because of what Jesus had said and done during his earthly ministry.

Jesus' followers were Jewish, and as they examined his life in the light of the Old Testament story, they came to the conclusion that Jesus really was the Son of God. It was an astounding thing to believe and preach, and to understand why they came to that conclusion we have to look more closely at what Jesus said and did while he was on earth.

ACTIONS SPEAK LOUDER THAN WORDS

John the Baptizer

In the Old Testament the prophets were traveling preachers who spoke the word of God. Like good actors they communicated by their actions as well as by their words. For example, a prophet named Hosea married a prostitute and was faithful to her even though she carried on with lots of other men. Through his own experience Hosea was trying to drive home the point that God was like a faithful husband and the people of Israel were like an unfaithful wife.

As part of his plan for the world, God prepared Jesus' cousin for a special ministry. This man's name was John and he was called "the Baptizer" because he called the Jewish people to turn away from their selfish ways and return to God. As a sign of their new inwardly clean condition he asked them to be publicly washed with water. This ceremonial washing was called *baptism*, from the Greek word *baptize*, which means "to wash."

Like Hosea, John was preaching with his actions as well as with his words. He wore rough clothes and lived in the desert as a sign of how terrible it was for people to live in the lonely wilderness of a life without God. To go out into the desert and be plunged into the fresh water was a sign that the person wanted to leave the desert of his sinful condition and enter a fresh, new kind of life.

But the baptism John offered also echoed an Old Testament ceremony. When the Old Testament king took his throne, the priest anointed him for his new role. The anointing ceremony was the public proclamation of the king's identity and duty in the community. The prophets were also anointed by God for their ministry. Oil poured on the head of the king or a prophet symbolized the blessing of God flowing down from heaven. This blessing was a recognition from heaven, and a gift of power to enable the prophet or king to perform his duties.

Christ: The Lamb of God

The greatest king of the Old Testament was the shepherd boy David. After his royal line came to an end, the prophets predicted that one day a new descendant of David would come and assume the throne. He would be a new kind of Shepherd-King. Because this King was specially chosen by God, he would have to be anointed as a sign of his special calling. The Hebrew term for the "anointed one" was *Messiah;* in Greek, *Christos,* from which we get the word *Christ.*

Once Jesus had grown up, we are told, he went out to the wilderness to see his cousin John preaching. John had been telling the people that someone greater was about to appear on the scene. The people were full of excitement and expectation. When Jesus appeared John pointed to him and said, "Behold the Lamb of God!"[9]

Remember, the people considered John to be a prophet, a special messenger from God himself. When he pointed to Jesus and said, "Behold the Lamb of God!" the people in the crowd understood that he was referring back to the Old Testament stories. The lamb that was killed in the Passover feast was also called the "Lamb of God." That lamb symbolically saved the people from death, and here was John saying that this unknown preacher called Jesus was the "Lamb of God." What could it mean?

[9] John 1:29.

Jesus then went to John to be baptized. When John poured the water on Jesus' head, it symbolized the anointing of the promised King. As a validation of the anointing John heard a voice from heaven saying, "This is my beloved Son, in whom I am well pleased."[10] Later on Jesus was given the name *Christ* because his followers remembered how his baptism was a kind of anointing by John. When John anointed Jesus he was recognizing that Jesus was the specially chosen Son of David who would be King. He was also recognizing Jesus as a specially blessed prophet and teacher. By calling him "the Lamb of God" he was also pointing to another, more mysterious dimension to Jesus' destiny.

Jesus the Good Teacher

Most everyone will agree that Jesus was a great religious teacher. As such, he ranks among the other great religious teachers in the world. Many of the things Jesus said are echoed in the words of other religious teachers. But while there are some similarities, there are also some big differences. Other religious teachers give their followers a plan or method to reach God. They teach a technique of prayer, a system of religious law, or a combination of both.

Jesus also teaches his followers to pray. However, his teaching on prayer is very simple. He doesn't teach difficult meditation techniques. He doesn't require you to undertake a course of study to master complicated religious language. Instead he teaches his followers to speak with God as a child speaks with his father.

Jesus also gives his followers a new kind of religious law, unlike any other religious system of dos and don'ts. It is the law of love. He tells his followers to forgive their enemies and to love those who do them harm. Jesus sums up all previous laws with two

[10]Matthew 3:17.

simple principles. First, love God. Second, love your neighbor as yourself. He says that all the religious laws in the world boil down to these two simple principles.

Jesus' teaching was so fresh and revolutionary that it turned the Jewish world upside down. But beyond the wisdom and simple freshness of his religious teachings is what they reveal about Jesus.

Jesus the Storyteller

One of the most famous ways Jesus taught people was with stories. The stories he told are called *parables*, and they are a unique form of story. They help people see how to live better lives. They show people what God is like, and like the rest of his teaching, they reveal who Jesus really is.

So, for example, Jesus told a series of stories about the final judgment. In one story a rich man gives his servants some money and asks them to invest it wisely. When he later asks for the money back, the servants have to answer for what they've done, and their responses vary, from that of the brilliant investor to the fool who made no profit at all.

In the story we see how to live wisely, but we also gain insight into God's character, for he is the one who gives the gifts for us to use. And the story also helps reveal who Jesus is, because elsewhere he tells another story about the final judgment, and there he is a shepherd judging between the sheep and the goats. (In Jesus' culture sheep and goats looked very similar, so judgment was difficult.) Taken together, those two stories reveal Jesus as one who gives us gifts and the one who judges how we have used them.

Lost and Found

Jesus also told a series of stories about things that were lost. A woman loses a valuable coin, a shepherd loses a sheep, and a father loses a runaway son. In each story the person who loses something precious searches relentlessly or waits patiently, and when it is restored there is great rejoicing all around.

The stories teach us to treasure the precious things in life, but they also show us a God who never tires in his search for his lost children. And then, when Jesus says *he* is one who comes to "seek and to save that which was lost,"[11] the stories take on a new level of meaning and point to his real identity.

These levels of meaning come together most powerfully in the story of the Good Shepherd who goes out to search for his lost sheep. The shepherd has a hundred sheep, but when he counts them at the end of the day, one is missing. He goes out into the wilderness to find the lost sheep and brings it home on his shoulders.

In the Old Testament the prophets had said that God was the Good Shepherd of his people, so the story confirms what God is like. But then Jesus says something that his hearers would have found shocking. He calls *himself* the Good Shepherd. In other words, Jesus is saying that the old promise that God himself would be the shepherd of his people is fulfilled in him.

Listen to My Actions

Jesus taught his disciples to pray. He taught them to love God. He told them stories about life. In all these ways he was also showing them who he really was. Like the prophets before him, Jesus taught not only through his words, but also through his actions. In what he said and what he did, Jesus pointed to the mystery of his true identity.

In this vein, the miracles of Jesus are not simply the party tricks of an amazing preacher. Neither are they just Jesus' way to show

[11]Luke 19:10.

that he had great power. Instead, the miracles of Jesus have a deeper meaning. They reveal who the miracle worker is.

When Jesus taught the people, they were amazed and said, "This man teaches with authority!" Jesus didn't disagree with them. Instead he said that his authority had been given by God himself. When Jesus healed people from sickness, he also forgave their sins. His enemies were shocked. They said, "Only God can forgive sins!" By forgiving people their sins, Jesus was making an astounding claim for himself.

When Jesus walked on the water and calmed the storm, he revealed who he really was. The Old Testament had said that the Lord God was he "who walks on the waves of the deep,"[12] so when Jesus walked on the waves, he was revealing that he was none other than the Lord of Creation.

It is true that Jesus was a good religious teacher, but his teachings and actions led his followers to conclude that he was more than just another religious teacher. Who was this religious teacher who had the nerve to claim to forgive sins and the power to calm the storm, heal the sick, and perform miracles to feed the hungry?

Jesus the Son of God

Through his stories, his teachings, and his actions, Jesus makes it clear that our relationship with God should be like that of a child with his Father.

But Jesus does more than teach us that we should be the children of God. In all his words and actions Jesus reveals what this new child-father relationship with God should be like. Furthermore, through his words and actions Jesus is telling us that he is not just *like* God's son. He *is* the Son of God.

---

[12]Job 9:8.

If Jesus had said, "My relationship with God is like that of a son to his father," we might accept that, but he goes further than that. He says, "I have come to do the will of my Father in heaven."[13] And "all authority in heaven and on earth has been given to me."[14]

This is where the teaching of Jesus is difficult. There are many people who think Jesus is a good teacher, but they pick out the nice and acceptable parts of Jesus' teaching and sidestep the parts that sound very strange and disturbing. In his stories and in his actions Jesus says that he and God are one. He says this in many ways, but finally he states it quite clearly. He not only says, "I have come to do the will of my Father." He says, "When you have seen me, you have seen the Father," and "I and the Father are one."[15]

WHO IS THIS MAN?

The Mystery Man

We wouldn't mind if Jesus were just a good religious teacher. We can accept his teachings about prayer and loving our neighbor. But can we really accept his claims to be the Son of God? We can accept that he was a good person — perhaps the greatest person who over lived. But can we really believe that he is God in human form?

Let's stop and consider for a moment. What kind of person was Jesus Christ? If you want to know, you should sit down sometime and read through one of the Gospels in one sitting. I guarantee that the Jesus you meet will be very different from the Jesus you thought you knew.

[13]Cf. John 6:38.
[14]Matthew 28:18.
[15]Cf. John 14:9; 10:30.

The God-Man

In the Gospels we meet a man who is complex and mysterious, and yet there is no trace of those twists in personality and contradictions of character that everyone else is prone to. Jesus goes through life with a clear purpose, and he stands out with a majestic simplicity and a quiet intensity that captivate and fascinate us.

He is religious, but never self-righteous. He is pure without being puritanical. He is magnificently good, but never "holier than thou." He is much sterner than the popular image of "gentle Jesus, meek and mild." But although he does not tolerate one scrap of evil, he is compassionate toward those who fall into sin. He is shrewd with intelligent people, but simple with more ordinary people. He seems modest, and yet he performs miracles and preaches powerfully. He is witty without being sarcastic and gentle without being weak. He is firm without being harsh, self-confident without being proud, and humble without being insecure. In every way he is balanced, mature, wise, sane, and humble.

Most important, in the Gospels we meet someone who is honest and real to his very core. He may be complex, but he is also transparent. There is no trace of guile, self-deceit, or vanity. Jesus is solid and down-to-earth. He doesn't strike us as a figure out of a story or a play. There is not an artificial or phony bone in his body. Instead he has all the honest unpredictability and complexity of a real person. He knows how the world of power and influence works, but he never schemes or kowtows to anyone. He is his own man, but he is not arrogant, eccentric, or proud.

When we meet Jesus in the Gospels, we are confronted with a person who strikes us as well adjusted. He knows who he is. He is whole. That is what we mean when we say that he is perfect. We don't simply mean that he never did anything wrong. We also mean that his personality doesn't have any weaknesses, faults, or kinks.

It is all that it should be. Jesus shows us what a perfect and complete human being looks like.

The Image of God

Yet even though he was perfectly human, even though he was fully divine (the Bible says he is the "image of the unseen God"[16]), he did not lord it over his followers. Indeed, elsewhere in the Bible it says that although Jesus was in the form of God, "he did not consider equality with God something to cling to, but he took the form of the servant."[17]

The Old Testament prophets pointed to the same truth. The prophet Isaiah said that the Christ would be a suffering *servant*. His purpose on earth was not to receive the accolades and enjoy the dominion that his perfection and divinity deserved, but to serve human beings by suffering for them.

Jesus is the suffering servant, the Good Shepherd, an anointed king, the "Son of Man" who, in the vision of the prophet Daniel, was as radiant and powerful as God himself sitting on a throne. In a powerful and irresistible way all the symbols and signs from the Old Testament and the New Testament come together like puzzle pieces falling into place. Each sign combines with the others to build up to the conclusion that Jesus Christ's astounding claims about himself might actually be true.

Big Problems

If this is so, then the teachings and life of Jesus present us with some big problems, because all the teachings and actions of Jesus consolidate the claims that he is the Son of God.

[16]Cf. Colossians 1:15.
[17]Cf. Philippians 2:6-7.

Many people believe that being a Christian basically means following Jesus' commandment to be good. They think it means being kind to others and trying not to lie, cheat, or steal. Of course Christians should not lie, cheat, or steal, but being a Christian is not simply a case of trying hard to be good. At the very heart of it all, being a Christian means we must come face-to-face with the astounding claims that Jesus Christ makes.

Put quite simply, Jesus Christ claims to be God in human form. What do we make of that? Presuming that the record we have of his words and deeds is accurate, then logically there are really only four choices.

First, what do we usually think if someone claims to be God? We think he's crazy. Now, it is possible that Jesus is crazy, but all the stories we have about him portray him as probably the most sane, down-to-earth, and realistic person who ever lived. If those stories are anything close to true, we can rule out this possibility. The Jesus we meet in the Gospels is not a crazy man, whatever else he might be.

The second choice is that Jesus is lying. Again, everything we know about him convinces us that if there was ever anyone honest through and through, it was this man. But let us suppose that he *was* a religious fraud. Maybe he was conning everyone. What was his motivation? There is no evidence that he gained either fame or fortune for his fraud. Indeed, he was always trying to escape from the crowds, and we know he lived in total poverty. In the end he gained nothing but pain and a terrible death. Very few frauds will go so far as to die for their lie.

The third choice is that Jesus' followers made a mistake. Perhaps they misunderstood his message. Maybe they thought he was God in human form, but he never intended them to think that. But we'd have to ask whether it is very likely that his followers would come up with such an outrageous suggestion. If they wanted to promote the message of Jesus, wouldn't it have made more sense to describe their friend as a great religious teacher? Once they said he was God, they made him sound not like a great religious teacher but like a madman or a fraud. In other words, even if Jesus did make such a claim, there was every reason for his followers to play it down and turn him into a good teacher instead of the Son of God — a claim that was far more outrageous, dangerous, and difficult to convince others of.

There is one other choice. If Jesus is not insane, if he is not a liar, and if his followers did not make a mistake about his claims, there is only one other choice: he was telling the truth, and he really is who he claims to be.

Who Do You Say I Am?

Jesus didn't allow people much leeway. He said we must choose. We are either for him or against him. We cannot serve two masters. We must decide whether Jesus really is God in human form.

We would like to defer the decision. We would like to withhold judgment, but by the nature of choice, this is impossible. We must choose, and not to choose is also to make a choice. If you are at a bus stop and a bus comes along, you may choose to get on or not. If you say you are not going to choose, then that is a choice not to get on the bus.

Before we make any decision we have to be clear about what the choices are. When we read the Gospels we have to consider the claims of Jesus. When we do, the option that Jesus was just a good teacher ceases to be viable. As we have seen, he is either God in human form, or he is a liar, or he is crazy, or his followers made a terrible mistake. He did not give us the option that he was just a good religious teacher.

Jesus forces this issue for an important reason. He wants us to understand that another guru is not what the human race needs. We don't need another system of good works or more techniques of meditation and prayer.

Earlier in the book we raised the difficult question of how God can be good yet allow suffering. Jesus understood that we need not only an intellectual answer to that question; we need someone to rescue us from the suffering each one of us must endure.

In one of his stories Jesus spoke about the shepherd who goes out on a lonely night to find just one lost sheep. He risks his own life to save that sheep and bring it home safely. When Jesus called himself the Good Shepherd he was saying that this is the reason he came: to seek and to save that which was lost.

Only God can put things right for the human race, and we can trust Jesus to help us put things right only if we believe that he has the power to do that. And we can believe that he has the power to do that only if we believe that he is God.

The extraordinary claims Jesus made about himself took him into the very heart of suffering. His claims got him into deep trouble. When Jesus was on trial he faced death because he claimed to be God. The Jewish leaders wouldn't have minded if he were just a good rabbi. They had lots of those. What they couldn't stand was that he claimed to have the power of God. So they killed him. Just as he presented them with a choice, so he presents us with the same choice. And it is a choice between life and death.

WHY DID HE DIE?

The Problem of Pain
Rather than ending, this is where the story really starts to get interesting. In the first section, I said that the question of how a

good God could allow suffering was the most important question in the world. I also said that Christianity is the religion that answers the question best. That's because Jesus didn't come to earth simply to give us an intellectual answer to a difficult exam question. God didn't take human form in Jesus simply to fill in the blank. Instead, he came to wrestle with the problem at the heart of his very being. In Jesus, God actually reaches down and embraces the terrible problem of evil and suffering in his own body.

The whole reason for Jesus' existence is summed up in the story of his temptation. After he was baptized by John, Jesus went out into the desert and ate nothing for forty days. While he was in the desert he endured a terrible assault by the Devil.

Wrestling with Demons

What do Christians believe about the Devil? Satan, or the Devil, is a real spiritual being. He is an angel who has fallen from his high condition because he wanted to be like God. Demons are other, lesser angels who have also fallen into the shadow side and seek to pervert God's way in the world.

Satan is also a symbol of death and destruction, violence and mayhem. He stands for the vast range of evil forces arrayed against all that is good. The Devil also represents the evil that each one of us struggles against. When he grappled with the Devil, Jesus was not just trying hard not to do anything bad. He was beginning a battle with evil that would last for the rest of his life.

His wrestling match with the Devil was a picture of what Jesus' whole life was really about. He did not come simply to teach people about God. He was not on earth just to heal people and teach them how to pray. His main purpose was to answer the problem of evil once and for all — by fighting a terrible battle against the Devil, to his very death.

The Unfair Advantage

If a good person fights against evil he will always be at a disadvantage. He will be fighting uphill. The good person has to engage with evil. He is not allowed to be a pacifist and sit on one side.

The evil person will naturally use every devious and nasty trick he can think of. That's why he's bad in the first place: he is a liar, a cheat, a murderer, and a thoroughgoing scoundrel. So the evil one will lie and scheme. He will punch below the belt and throw salt in the good guy's eyes.

But the really good person is not allowed to lower himself to dirty tricks. Jesus actually taught this principle. When our enemy slaps us we are told to turn the other cheek. When our enemy takes our coat we are to offer him our shirt as well.

This disadvantage that the good person suffers is actually the key that unlocks the whole mystery. You see, evil gets worse and worse in the world when we do not fight it with goodness. We usually respond to suffering by causing more suffering. We seek revenge and return evil for evil.

When we do this, evil breeds in the world and can never be defeated. That is why Jesus teaches us to return good for evil, to forgive our enemies, and to pray for those who hurt us. Jesus is trying to get across to us that the only way for evil to be defeated is to smother it with goodness, as water puts out a fire.

The Sacrificial Lamb

That sounds neat and tidy. It's not. We forget how evil the enemy really is. If we turn the other cheek and refuse to fight evil with more evil, then by the very nature of that decision we will become victims of evil. Those who are violent will have no qualms about squashing good people underfoot. Therefore the stark answer to the problem of evil seems to be that the forces of evil must trample the good person down, and the good person must become an innocent victim.

In the Old Testament religion, this is what the sacrifice of an innocent lamb was supposed to symbolize. The pure little lamb did nothing wrong. He was put forward as a symbol of innocence in the face of evil. He was unable to fight against evil, so the evil forces would devour him. He would be slaughtered and die.

When the Jews celebrated Passover they actually slaughtered the "Lamb of God" and daubed its blood on their doorways so that the powers of death would pass over their homes and they would be delivered. In a symbolic way they believed the innocent lamb took the evil of the world into itself. Evil was absorbed into goodness, even if it meant that the goodness would have to die and the light would have to be put out.

Jesus Turns the Tables on Evil

All of this is summed up and fulfilled when Jesus is given the title (by John the Baptist) "Lamb of God." Because he is good, Jesus must battle against evil. But because he is good, he is not able to fight evil with evil. He cannot return violence for violence. As a result, the violent will bear him away.

The battle against evil is grim, and the price is great. When Jesus is betrayed by a friend, condemned by a crooked court, and crucified with criminals, he shows us that real goodness is devoured by evil. There is no other way. Because the evil one cheats, lies, and uses violence, he wins.

But at the very darkest point, the tables are turned. The Jewish people celebrated the Passover as a celebration of liberation, not as a memorial of defeat. Through the Passover events they came out of slavery and began their journey to the land of prosperity and promise.

In the same way, when Jesus is trampled down and finally killed by the powers of evil, the tables are turned. Although evil wins the battle, good will win the war.

When faced with the darkest evil, we must always remember something that the evil ones always forget: that evil has no real power of itself. Evil is only good that has been twisted and perverted. At the heart of evil is a dark void. Because evil is nothing positive in itself, it cannot possibly triumph in the end. Likewise, because goodness is positive and powerful, it must finally prevail. Darkness may seem overwhelming, but darkness is nothing in itself. It is simply the absence of light. Therefore even the smallest amount of light must banish the dark.

The powers of evil might have been able to snuff the light of Christ, but they could not put out the light forever. How could evil *really* win? It is impossible, for evil (because it is a twisted good) actually relies on goodness for its very existence. If evil were to win, if the Devil could kill God, he would be cutting off the branch he was sitting on. Because evil is dependent on good for its existence, if good is vanquished, evil itself would also cease to exist.

It was inevitable that Jesus would be trampled by the powers of evil, but he couldn't have stayed dead no matter what his enemies did to him. Because Jesus was God, and because of his overwhelming goodness, he had to rise again just as surely as the rooster has to crow and just as surely as the sun will rise each morning. Goodness had to prevail. That is how the whole system is written.

The death and resurrection of Jesus are therefore the ultimate answer to the question of suffering and a good God. Because he is good, God creates a universe where freedom exists. This means evil is a possibility. Evil twists the natural order. It distorts what is good. As a result terrible suffering follows. This suffering goes in a downward spiral away from goodness, away from what is natural, and away from God. But because God is good, he himself provides the solution, even though it costs him everything.

A Cause to Celebrate

This is why Christians celebrate Holy Week (including Good Friday, the day on which Jesus died) and Easter as the most important part of the year. Each year we celebrate the fact that Jesus Christ defeated evil, not with the tools of evil, but by his overwhelming goodness — even though that meant his own terrible death.

On Easter we celebrate the historical fact that Jesus could not stay dead. Death could not hold him. He was too alive, too good, and too powerful for that. His ultimate sacrifice meant that he embraced death and evil and simply squeezed them to death with his overwhelming love and goodness. That's why he rose from the dead, because there was simply no more death to hold him.

This is the heart of the Christian faith. To become a Christian we don't just listen to Jesus and try to be good. Instead we come to understand the meaning of his death and resurrection, and we participate in that victory. When people become Christian they accept what Jesus' death means and they are baptized as a symbolic way of entering into solidarity with that death.

This is also what Christian worship is all about. We don't go to church just to meet our friends, sing hymns, and hear the good teachings of Jesus. We go to participate in his victory over evil. Through the church ceremony of the *Mass*, or the *Eucharist*, Jesus' death and resurrection come alive in the present moment and we relive them with Christ.

At that point we celebrate the amazing fact that the eternal riddle of evil and a good God has been answered once and for all.

The war is over. The victory is won. All that remains is for us to sign the peace treaty and put it into force.

WHAT DID HE ACHIEVE?

The Second Adam

When the first Christians reflected on the death of Jesus they came to some revolutionary conclusions. As Jews, the followers of Jesus considered Adam to be a representative of the whole human race. The word *Adam* means "man," so when they said Adam was created in the image of God the ancient writers meant all of mankind was created in God's image. If Jesus really was a new and even fuller image of God in human form, then it was right to call him (as the Bible does) "the second Adam."[18]

According to the story, the first Adam brought death and suffering into the world by his disobedience, but the second Adam (Jesus) defeated death and suffering through his total obedience to God's will. The New Testament says Jesus was obedient "even to death on the cross."[19] Through his terrible death Jesus wrestled with suffering and death for the whole human race.

It is difficult for us to put ourselves into the same mind-set as these first Christians two millennia ago. We think individualistically and find it difficult to understand how one person can represent the whole human race. It's quite sensible to ask, "How can the death of Jesus affect me two thousand years later?"

Yet in political terms we can all understand how a head of state such as a queen or a president can represent the whole nation. Also, scientists tell us that we have all descended from the same

[18]Cf. 1 Cor. 15:45.
[19]Cf. Philippians 2:8.

genetic parents. In one sense we really are all connected. We are all brothers and sisters in the human race. If this is so, then any human could stand in for the whole human race.

But God didn't choose just any person to represent humanity. He chose the person who was a whole and complete and perfect human being. Because he was whole and complete as a human being, Jesus Christ held in himself each one of us. So when he embraced suffering and death he really was embracing the suffering and death of each one of us.

Justice and Mercy

It is very difficult for us to conceive how the death of Jesus can touch us. But there are many ways to think about it. Saying that Jesus represents the whole human race is one way. But we can also think about where we were headed and what it took to turn us around.

Because of our twisted human condition, all of us are on the road away from God rather than toward him. This, by its very nature, means we are headed for disaster. It is not so much that God is punishing us because we are naughty little children. Instead, our punishment is built into our decision. Each choice to disobey God has within it the choice to be separated from him forever. If we go our own way we mustn't be surprised if we end up far away from God.

God realizes that we are headed away from him, and he doesn't want us to end up in such a disaster. But because God is good, he must also be just. He can't just take away the natural results of our bad choices; otherwise the choices themselves would be meaningless. So God has to allow justice to take its course.

But because God is good, he is not only just; he is also merciful. Therefore God must make sure that justice is done while mercy is exercised. So in a brilliant stroke, God has seen fit for his own Son to offer the human race both justice and mercy at the same time.

When Jesus died on the Cross Christians believe that God himself took the just punishment for our disobedience and offered us mercy in return. It is not that Jesus died in our place to satisfy an angry God. Instead Jesus stepped in to make God's justice effective while he also offered mercy. Part of this mercy means that, if we want to, we can turn away from our selfish path through life, accept what Jesus has done for us, and turn back toward God.

Forgiveness Forever

Another way of talking about God's mercy and justice is with the term *forgiveness*. We often think of forgiveness as simply excusing somebody for an injury. So when someone steps on our toe we say, "Don't worry. I forgive you."

But when we are hurt badly, forgiveness isn't so easy. The person who stepped on our toe didn't mean to hurt us. It was an accident. But if someone steps on our toe deliberately time and again, we do not forgive quite so easily. If we do forgive, we are right to demand restitution. If the person has broken our toe we might forgive him, but we still want him to pay the doctor's bill.

When Jesus died on the Cross Christians believe he won God's forgiveness for all of us. He did this by paying the price of our forgiveness, and that price was the death and suffering that was required for evil to be defeated forever.

Christians therefore say that "Jesus died to save us" or "Jesus died to forgive us." This is what it means in theory, but this is also what it means in reality. The forgiveness and mercy Jesus won on the Cross really are available for individual people. The way to obtain this forgiveness is the way we always obtain forgiveness: by asking for it with a sincere heart.

Good, Bad, or Forgiven?

This is the simple and astounding truth: Christianity is not foremost about being good. It is about being forgiven. The only precondition for becoming a Christian is not that you be a saint, but that you be a sinner. A Christian comes to realize who Jesus Christ is, and what he has accomplished through his death and resurrection. Once he has realized this, he uses various means to connect with that death and resurrection and claim the results of it for himself.

The simplest way to do this is simply to face facts and say to yourself, "I have been living my life my way. It hasn't brought me real happiness. I want to live life God's way." Then we need to tell God so: "Dear God, I want to live life your way. I want to claim forgiveness and mercy from Jesus Christ. Please help me."

At its heart, this is what it means to be a Christian: to hear the call of Christ and decide to follow him. Down through the ages this simple decision has been made by billions of people, from little children to the elderly. Sometimes they have done so with great emotion and felt a huge surge of love and new life. Other times they have done so with quiet confidence and simple trust. However they have done it, these billions of people of every race, language, and tribe down through the ages have simply heard the call of Jesus Christ, and they have dropped what they were doing, turned from their own way, and followed him.

Transformed into His Likeness

It is true that Jesus calls us to follow him, but he also says, "You cannot be my follower unless you take up your cross and follow me."[20] In other words, following Jesus means not just trying to

[20] Cf. Luke 14:27.

live by his teachings, but trying to imitate his sacrificial actions. Jesus wants us to live in union with him and to live his life in the world.

This means we are called to be transformed people. Christians are not just following religious laws and techniques for prayer and meditation in order to be better people. They are seeking to be totally and utterly transformed into the image and likeness of Jesus Christ.

He shows us humanity at its richest and fullest potential. To be like him, therefore, is for each one of us to become all that we can be, and, while remaining ourselves, to be re-created into the image of God — just as God first intended.

This is where forgiveness leads us: to a basic turnaround from walking our own way to walking God's way. Walking our own way is like a downward spiral into nothingness. Walking God's way is an upward climb into the fullest and richest life imaginable. This climb isn't easy, but it is the goal we were created for, and unless we are on this upward climb, we are not becoming all we can be.

Just as Jesus was the God-Man, so when he calls us to be like him, the call is to be no less than little God-men and -women. The New Testament puts it another way. It says our ultimate destiny is to be brothers and sisters of Christ — the adopted sons and daughters of God. The exciting news is that he has also given us the power to accomplish this transformation.

Theory and Practice

This is not just nice religious talk. This is not just theory. It is practice. It can really happen, and this complete transformation of individuals into little godlike beings is the whole point of the Christian religion. In order for this to happen, Jesus Christ established a practical way for us to become one with him and for this transformation of ourselves, and eventually the whole human race, to begin.

To accomplish this, Jesus did four things. First, he set up a community of like-minded people. Everyone who wanted to join this community had go through the initiation ritual of Baptism. In this ceremony they declared their desire to turn from their own way, they expressed their belief in Christ, and they vowed to join his continuing fight against evil in the world.

Second, Jesus established a basic ceremony through which this community would always remember his death, because (as we have seen) his suffering and death were the heart of the whole matter. Through this ritual Jesus promised to remain with his followers forever and to fill their lives with his own life and power.

Third, Jesus set up a visible and historical structure for this community. It was simple in its design. Initially, twelve men would be leaders by Christ's own appointment. As the community grew, they would appoint successors. So they would know who was in charge, Jesus chose one of those men, named Peter, to stand in Christ's place as the main leader.

Finally, he promised to be with his followers until the end of time. To do this he sent his own Spirit into the world to be the Life Force of this fledgling community. The exciting way that great Holy Spirit transforms our lives and changes the world is the subject of the next chapter.

Chapter Three

The Fire of Life

JESUS KEEPS HIS PROMISE

Let's not mince words. Christians believe that Jesus Christ rose from the dead. We believe this astounding twist in the plot really happened. It wasn't a make-believe happy fairytale ending. It was a real, physical, historical event. It surprised everyone and changed the course of human history forever.

Many people simply cannot believe in Jesus' resurrection and honestly admit they're not Christians. Others want to be Christian, but just can't accept that the resurrection *really* happened. So they attempt to "re-interpret" the resurrection event, and say something like, "Jesus didn't physically rise from the dead. Instead, Jesus' *memory* continued to live on within the lives of his followers."

This is another way of saying that the resurrection is simply a beautiful idea. But if the resurrection didn't happen, that idea has no meaning. It's like saying marriage is a beautiful thing, as long as you don't actually live together or make love. But if you don't live together and make love, then a marriage is not a marriage, and it is not even a beautiful idea; it is not anything at all.

For marriage to have meaning, it has to be physical. Likewise, for the resurrection to have meaning, it had to have happened. After all, that's what resurrection *means*: someone rose from the dead, never to die again. It's no good pretending that it was just a beautiful idea. One of the great early Christian apostles, a man named Paul, said that if Jesus didn't truly rise from the dead, then the faith of those who followed him was in vain.

Did It Really Happen?

Stop for a moment and think it through. If Jesus Christ rose from the dead, it is literally the most important event in human history.

If we want to think about this event fairly, we must take a serious look at the events recorded in the Gospels. Even if the resurrection of Jesus sounds incredible, we must consider the possibility fair and square. It is vital to do so, because if Jesus did not really rise from the dead, he was only a good teacher, and if he is only a good teacher, he does not have the power to deliver us from death. And if he does not have that power, he is not the solution to the problem of suffering and death.

Consider the story: The Gospel writers go out of their way to make it clear that the resurrection of Jesus really happened. The gospels were written within the lifetime of eyewitnesses. They report that many people saw Jesus die on the Cross and be buried, and that days later the same people saw him walking and talking in their midst.

These eyewitnesses touched Jesus. They saw him eat food. They put their fingers in his open wounds. Certain details of the story might have been altered slightly in the telling, but because eyewitnesses were still living when the Gospels were written, we can trust that the Gospel writers did not invent the story, nor alter the events substantially.

When they discovered the empty tomb on Easter morning, Jesus' followers ran away in terror. That shows us just how real, frightening, and earth-shattering an event this was. Would they have invented such an unbelievable story? In general terms, the more fantastic a story is, the more unlikely it is that people have made it up. The fact that these men and women were later prepared to die for their version of events makes us conclude that something stupendous really did happen to them.

A World Turned Upside Down

The disciples had their world turned upside down. Once they realized what it meant, they were overwhelmed, and we should be, too, for the resurrection means that history is changed forever.

Human history is changed because, if Jesus rose from the dead, it means that the great enemy, death, can be beaten at last. If the resurrection only means that Jesus continued to live in the memory of his followers, then victory over death is just a bright idea — no more than religious wishful thinking. If there is no victory over death, then the Christian faith is just another religious system of prayer and good works like all the others.

However, if Jesus really rose from the dead, if he conquered evil and death, maybe I can, too. Maybe the whole world can be transformed by that same power.

The Christian faith is about that very possibility, and the apostle Paul was so sure of it that he cried out, "Death, where is your sting? Grave, where is your victory?"[21]

Up, Up, and Away

After Jesus had risen from the dead he continued to teach his twelve Apostles for a time. Then he said that he had to go away, but promised that he would be with them until the end of time. To

---

[21]Cf. 1 Corinthians 15:55.

remain with them he would send a "Comforter," the "Spirit of Truth."[22] This Spirit would "lead them into all truth" and "teach them all things."[23] The Spirit of Truth would come to help them, but they needed human leadership, too, so Jesus asked Peter, the leader of the Apostles, to take that role.

After he had risen from the dead, Jesus could not live forever on this earth. If he remained on earth his enemies would have kept on trying to kill him. But if he just disappeared, people would assume he had wandered off to die someplace quietly. If he faded away or vanished from their sight, they would conclude that he hadn't risen from the dead physically, but that they had seen a ghost.

Jesus had to go away, but in order to make it clear that he had really physically risen from the dead, and that he was not going to die again, he had to go to the spiritual realm in a visibly physical way. Jesus therefore made sure that his followers saw him physically depart from this earth.

Forty days after he had risen from the dead, he took his Apostles to a hill outside Jerusalem. He gave them his own authority and power and told them to continue his work. To confirm his promise Jesus said his Spirit would help them to do his work in the world. Then he rose up, and they watched him go from their sight.

Is it difficult to believe that Jesus rose from earth to heaven? If you accept that Jesus is who he says he is (God in human form), it makes sense that he would not be able to stay dead. It also follows that once he had risen from the dead, he would need to go away in a physical manner.

Jesus' disappearance into a cloud sounds like a fantasy story, but how else could it have happened? We know that heaven is not a

[22]Cf. John 14:16, 17.
[23]Cf. John 16:13; 14:26.

big golden city on the other side of the clouds. Heaven is a spiritual realm. But because Jesus had to be seen to move physically to the spiritual realm, the spiritual realm had to be located somewhere, and the sky is the best symbol we have for the spiritual realm.

But Jesus didn't leave this earth for heaven simply to tie up the loose ends of the story. His return to heaven was also the completion of his destiny. By going to heaven as a human being he opened up the way for us to follow. By returning to heaven he took his place in that realm as the victorious hero returning home.

The Fire and Wind Come Down

After Jesus had gone to the spiritual realm, his followers waited in Jerusalem. The Bible tells us that they prayed and worshiped together along with Mary, the mother of Jesus, and others who had witnessed the resurrection. The Apostles were the ones Jesus had specially chosen, and Peter was their leader, just as Christ had requested.

While they waited for the gift Jesus had promised, the Apostles remembered Jesus through the simple memorial meal, as he had commanded them. When he had celebrated the ancient Jewish Passover feast with them just before his death, Jesus had said the bread was his body and the wine was his blood. The Apostles believed that, in a miraculous way beyond human understanding, the bread and wine at this meal really did become the body and blood of Christ. In this way Jesus was present with them just as he promised he would be. As they ate the bread and drank the wine that had become the body and blood of Christ, they became part of Jesus and he became a part of them.

At this time — just over forty days after the Passover festival — the Apostles, along with Jews from all around the world, had gathered in Jerusalem for another Jewish festival called Pentecost. Pentecost marked the end of the Passover season and the beginning of the harvest season. Pentecost was also a celebration of God's revelation (the Ten Commandments) to Moses on Mount Sinai. At Sinai God's presence was manifested in an earthquake, wind, and fire.

As a fulfillment of this event the Apostles also experienced an astounding manifestation of God's presence. Suddenly, as they were together, there was the sound of a mighty wind, and flames of fire appeared over the heads of the Apostles and their followers.

The little group of Jesus' followers felt a surge of power within them. This experience must have been overwhelming, because it is recorded that they were so affected by this supernatural infilling of the Holy Spirit that observers joked that they were drunk. Then Peter stood up and got everyone's attention. He said his friends weren't drunk, as it was only nine o'clock in the morning. Instead, they were filled with the Holy Spirit, just as Jesus had promised.

Powerful Preaching

On that day, Peter preached with astounding power and insight. Before these events he had been cowardly and confused. Now he was a powerful leader. The gift Jesus had promised had really come upon him. Peter told the Jewish people gathered there about Jesus, who had been killed, but had risen again. He reminded them that many people had seen Jesus alive, and that Jesus had risen again because it was simply impossible for death to hold him. He quoted passages from the Jewish religious writings to show the Jews how Jesus had fulfilled their ancient prophecies. Then he declared that the resurrection proved that Jesus was exactly who he said he was: the Jewish Messiah, the anointed servant of God, the very Son of God.

Then Peter delivered the final thrust. He told the Jewish leaders that they had crucified their own Messiah. Many people were swayed by Peter's powerful preaching and asked what they had to do. He answered, "Repent and be baptized in the name of Jesus Christ, for the forgiveness of sins, and you will receive the gift of the Holy Spirit."[24]

At that moment the essence of the Christian religion became clear. Human beings might have killed the one who was sent to save them, but, through their very actions, he was nevertheless able to accomplish what he was sent for. Human evil might have been great, but God's love was greater. By allowing himself to be a victim of evil, Jesus Christ defeated evil and death forever and was able to offer a share in his victory to all people.

Peter says that we are able to join ourselves with Christ's victory in three simple steps. First, we have to realize that, even though part of us wants to do good, all of us have chosen the selfish way in life. We have hurt ourselves and others. If we had been there in Jerusalem that fateful week, we probably would have consented to Jesus' death, or at least stood silent and done nothing about it. Once we realize that we are on the side of evil, we must be sorry for the fact.

The second step is to switch sides. We must decide to live life God's way, not our way. Furthermore, we must accept that it is through Jesus' death and resurrection that we have the power to make this decision and stick with it.

Third, as a sign of our decision, we must be plunged into water while invoking God the Father, Jesus his Son, and the Holy Spirit. By this physical action our inner decision to change is put into action. By this process we are washed clean spiritually and enter into

[24]Cf. Acts 2:38.

Jesus' life. The wrong things we have done are forgiven, and we receive the Spirit that Jesus had promised.

Through this threefold action the New Testament says we are "born again"[25] and given a fresh start in life as members of God's family.

Anyone can begin this process at any time. If you have understood this simple core of the Christian faith, as you read this, you can take the first two steps — being sorry and switching sides — right now. All it takes is for you to speak to God, saying that you are sorry, that you believe Jesus Christ died and rose again for your sake, and that you want to change your life. If you have already been baptized, then, by making this decision, you have begun to claim what was done for you in Baptism. If you have not been baptized, you need to search out your local Catholic Church and talk to a priest, who will help you take the next step.

Twelve Timid Men

Did the events of Pentecost really happen? After all, there have been similar stories of mighty winds, supernatural flames, and people speaking in strange heavenly languages right down to the present day. But these supernatural, religious events are not the best evidence that something amazing occurred in Jerusalem that day.

Something stupendous must have happened because of the historical and human results. Before Pentecost Peter was a coward. The night Jesus was arrested and taken away, Peter had denied that he even knew Jesus. The other apostles weren't much better. They were confused, frightened, ordinary men who were unsure of themselves and unsure of who Jesus really was.

[25]Cf. John 3:3.

What happened to transform these twelve timid men into religious leaders who spearheaded a movement that eventually challenged the Roman Empire and transformed human history? Peter was ready to run away, but in the end, he led the first Christians to stand up courageously for the truth, and later died a martyr's death. What happened to turn Peter from a weak coward into a powerful and fearless world leader who would eventually go to Rome and lay down his life for his beliefs?

The resurrection and ascension of Jesus released the power that came down at Pentecost. The three events are dependent on each other. The same power that raised Jesus from the dead was suddenly available to transform ordinary people's lives. The religious experiences of others ever since that momentous day in Jerusalem have proven that weak, ordinary people really can be transformed by this resurrection force.

Peter's is just one example of a life transformed. There are countless others. Francis of Assisi was a confused young soldier home from the wars, but he was converted from a spoiled dreamer of a rich boy into the founder of a powerful religious order that changed the world.

Mother Teresa was just an ordinary nun teaching in a convent school, but the same power that transformed Peter and Francis of Assisi turned her into a spiritual dynamo who established an international movement. She went on to challenge presidents and prime ministers with her message of the preciousness of human life. Karol Wojtyla was an ordinary young student, but God's power transformed him into Pope John Paul the Great — a man who changed the course of history.

The conversion experiences described in the New Testament are echoed in millions of ordinary lives down through history. The evidence of transformed lives is everywhere, and if it happened to

Peter and Francis of Assisi and Mother Teresa and Pope John Paul, it can happen to you and to me, too.

A Global Vision

This is how Jesus planned to transform the whole world: by transforming individuals who would change the world. He said that a seed cannot grow unless it first falls into the ground and dies. He also said that his kingdom is like a tiny seed that is planted, then grows into a huge tree, full of life and power.

Jesus was the little seed that died and was buried. His resurrection was the growth and blossoming of that great tree. The gift of the Holy Spirit is like its life-giving sap. The whole family of Christ's followers down through the ages is like the tree that is growing to provide shelter and shade for the whole world.

At Pentecost God's plan for the renewal and transformation of the world became clear. By his death and resurrection, Jesus Christ released a power into the world that would continue to work through the world, as current surges through an electrical system. This force is always there, working to bring about new life; to rescue all that is soiled and dying, and bring it to a fresh, new beginning. Furthermore, the same creative Spirit that was released at Pentecost had been active from the beginning of time.

THE TRANSFORMING POWER OF THE SPIRIT

The Spirit of Creation

At Pentecost humanity experienced the spiritual equivalent of a huge volcanic eruption. Forces that had been bubbling beneath the surface suddenly burst out with enormous power. Before Pentecost God's Spirit was also surging and working in the world, but in a more general way. When Jesus came, the work of the Spirit came into focus. When Jesus died and rose again he released God's powerful Spirit into the world in a more specific way.

Because the Holy Spirit was at work in the world from the very beginning, it is worth looking to the past to see how and what he did. The Spirit's work is recorded in the Old Testament, which is the first half of the Bible. By looking at how the Holy Spirit worked in the Old Testament we can understand how the Spirit is focused in the life and teaching of Jesus Christ. Seeing this will then help us to understand how the Spirit can transform our lives today.

At the beginning of the Bible the Jewish people recorded their ancient creation story. They were not giving a scientific and historical account of the beginning of the world. Instead, in simple, poetic language they described how God was the source of all things from the beginning. In majestic words they said, "In the beginning God created the heavens and the earth, and the earth was without form. It was empty, and the breath of God moved over the surface of the deep watery chaos."[26]

Two pictures come together in these ancient words. One is the image of a great bird hovering over the watery chaos. That shadowy presence was there from the beginning as the creative power behind all things. The other image is of "God's breath." By breathing over the watery darkness God brought life into existence.

This "hovering spirit" or "breath of God" can also be understood as the "Spirit of God." In other words, God's Holy Spirit was there at the beginning, as the creative force in the world. Later in the creation story this same spirit brings man to life because God "breathes into Adam the breath of life."[27]

[26]Cf. Genesis 1:1-2.
[27]Cf. Genesis 2:7.

Jesus and the Creator Spirit

At the creation the Holy Spirit, like a great hovering bird, brought new life out of the waters of chaos. The same image was echoed at the baptism of Jesus. When he came up out of the water he saw the Spirit like a dove hovering over him. The symbolism is the same: the Spirit is present to bring forth a new kind of spiritual life.

Just as the "breath of God" brought creation into being, and breathed life into the first human, so after his resurrection Jesus breathed on his Apostles and said, "Receive the Holy Spirit."[28] This is a symbol that they were being re-created and that humanity was getting a fresh start with a new breath of God.

It is no coincidence that at Pentecost the followers of Jesus heard the sound of a mighty rushing wind. The creative breath that Jesus had blown on his Apostles in a symbolic way was the same breath of God that had blown over the world at the beginning of creation. The same Spirit of new life is now available to breathe new life into our stale, confused existence. The Spirit that brought creation out of chaos is actively seeking to create order out of the chaos of our lives.

The Spirit of Liberty

The Spirit's character is revealed by what the Spirit does. In the Old Testament one of the things God's Spirit does is liberate slaves and deliver from death. The story of Exodus reveals how God's Spirit saved the Jewish people from death and brought them into freedom from their slavery in Egypt.

Moses was a young Jewish man who had been brought up in the court of the Egyptian pharaoh. After killing an Egyptian who

[28]John 20:22.

was striking a fellow Jew, Moses had to flee for his life into the wilderness. In the desert he married and settled down to live as a nomadic shepherd.

Then one day, as he was tending his sheep, Moses was startled by a vision of a bush on fire. When he looked closer, he saw that, although the bush was burning, it was not being consumed by the flames.

Moses heard a voice that seemed to come from within the bush. The voice said that it was the God of his Jewish ancestors, and that Moses was destined to return to Egypt to lead the Jews out of slavery to freedom in their own land.

Eventually Moses obeyed. In Egypt the Spirit delivered the Jewish people from terrible plagues and a sure death. When they were finally released the Jewish people were led on their journeys by a cloud that was like a pillar of fire. The burning bush and the cloudy pillar of fire were powerful symbols of the Holy Spirit. The fire brought light and warmth and led them into freedom.

Jesus and the Fire of Freedom

John the Baptist's message was also about freedom from slavery and death. He announced that someone greater than he would soon appear. John said, "I have baptized with water, but one is coming who will baptize you with the Holy Spirit and with fire."[29] Then Jesus appeared and was baptized by John.

Straight after his baptism Jesus went out into the desert, where he went through a time of spiritual testing. Then he went to his hometown of Nazareth and announced his mission. He went into the synagogue (which was the local Jewish church) and read a passage from the Old Testament prophet Isaiah that said, "The Spirit

[29]Cf. Matthew 3:11.

of the Lord is upon me, because he has anointed me to preach good news to the poor. He has sent me to proclaim release to the captives and recovering of sight to the blind, to set at liberty those who are oppressed."[30]

Everyone stared at him. What could he mean? The passage that Jesus had read referred to the expected servant of God, the Anointed One — the Messiah.

Then, to their amazement, Jesus said with complete confidence, "Today this prophecy is fulfilled in your hearing."[31] Just as the Holy Spirit had led the Jews out of slavery, Jesus claimed to have a special calling to do the same thing.

Jesus' ministry was only the start. When the tongues of fire appeared on the day of Pentecost, God was using the same symbol of fire to show that the Spirit who had liberated the Jewish people from slavery in Egypt was now given to deliver people from slavery to their twisted selfish nature.

Each one of us is enslaved by some sort of addiction or weakness. The fiery energy force that delivered the Jewish people is now available to us. The Holy Spirit can help deliver us from the slavery of our addictions; he can liberate us from our fears and our selfishness and lead us to a new spiritual life — a life that is abundant and free.

The Spirit of Wisdom

The Jewish people finally came into their Promised Land, and eventually a king was chosen to rule over them. King David consolidated the kingdom and established peace and prosperity. He was succeeded by his son Solomon.

[30]Cf. Isaiah 61:1; Luke 4:18.
[31]Cf. Luke 4:21.

During this time the different civilizations around Israel had started to write down their wise sayings — "quotable quotes" that helped people to get on in life. The Jewish people, too, developed their own forms of "wisdom literature." They added drama, poetry, and stories to the quotable quotes to have memorable ways of passing their wisdom from one generation to the next. Solomon was considered the wisest king of the time because he was a master of this kind of practical wisdom.

Eventually the Jewish people came to understand that wisdom was not only practical advice for dealing with life's problems. If a person really wanted to be wise, he would have to ask the big questions about life: Why are we here? Is there a God? Why must we die? How can God be good yet allow suffering?

The Jews realized that people couldn't answer these questions on their own. The big questions are so difficult to answer, and there was so much disagreement, that the Jews realized they needed to have the truth revealed to them by a higher power. They visualized a "Spirit of Wisdom" that led them to enlightenment and spiritual understanding.

Wisdom and Wave Walking

The Gospel of Luke tells us on two occasions that as a boy Jesus "grew in wisdom."[32] Luke doesn't simply mean that Jesus was getting a good education. Luke understood from the Old Testament that *Wisdom* was another name for the Holy Spirit.

Jesus' connection to God's holy Wisdom, or Spirit, continues throughout the Gospels. For example, the Jews thought of the sea as a dangerous and chaotic place. In some Old Testament passages God is the one who calms the sea and walks on the waves, and in

---

[32] Cf. Luke 2:40, 52.

one of the Old Testament wisdom poems, it is Wisdom who "walks on the waves of the sea."[33]

In the Gospels Jesus calms a storm, and in one story he actually comes to his followers by walking across the waves. These stories were not told simply to impress people with Jesus' ability to perform miracles. The Gospel writers told the stories to make people consider who Jesus really was: the one in whom God's Spirit lived.

The people who first heard these stories knew who had the power to calm the storm and walk on the waves. So when Jesus performed these powerful actions his followers rightly asked the question, "Who is this man?"

They knew from the Old Testament that God is the one who brings creation out of watery chaos. God is the one who calms the storm, and it is the Holy Spirit of Wisdom who walks on the waves of the sea. Since Jesus calmed the storm and walked on the waves, the first Christians concluded that Jesus was the Wisdom of God in human form.

When Jesus sent his Spirit onto individuals at Pentecost they realized that the same Spirit of Wisdom who had led the ancient Jews to understand the Truth was also with them to lead and guide them into all truth. That same Spirit of Wisdom is available to each one of us. All we need to do is ask for it.

Tapping into the Power

Throughout the history of the Jewish people the Spirit of creation continued to bring them into new life. The same Spirit continued to lead them into freedom whenever they fell back into the slavery of selfish, destructive behavior. Through their poets,

---

[33]Cf. Sirach 24:5-6.

priests, and preachers the Spirit continued to teach them and bring them to new insights and understandings about themselves and God.

By the work of the Holy Spirit the Jews were being prepared for the coming of Jesus, and through their history, God would open up the whole world to a fresh understanding of his goodness and truth. When Jesus came he did the same things in a specific way that the Holy Spirit had done within the history of the Jewish people.

Jesus brought new life. He said, "I have come that you may have life in all its fullness."[34] Jesus also brought freedom. By healing people he delivered them from the bondage of ill health. By forgiving their sins he delivered them from guilt, fear, and darkness. Jesus also taught them the truth about God and so led them in the paths of real wisdom.

But Jesus was not just full of the Holy Spirit, as another religious leader might be. He was actually *one* with the Holy Spirit. Likewise, Jesus did not simply teach people about God the Father. He said, "I and the Father are one."[35]

In other words, Jesus is the connecting point between God the Father and the Holy Spirit. He is also the junction point between us and God. This unity between Jesus, the Holy Spirit, and the Father is vital, because it shows us where we can get the power needed for our lives to be transformed.

Jesus does not just teach us about God and the Holy Spirit. He takes us into real, powerful contact with God. To understand how this happens, we have to understand better how Jesus, the Father, and the Holy Spirit live and work as one.

[34] Cf. John 10:10.
[35] John 10:30.

Christianity Pure and Simple

Why the Holy Trinity?

Probably the most unusual and difficult belief Christians hold is the idea that the one God is a *Trinity* of persons: Father, Son, and Holy Spirit. It makes sense to many people that there is only one God. They quite rightly say that God is a total and utter mystery, ultimately beyond our powers of understanding or description. They wonder, then, why we have to bother with such a difficult and seemingly contradictory concept as the Trinity.

One of the reasons we "bother" is because we believe that Trinity is what God has revealed himself to be. As the first Christians began to think about the way God worked in the world, they came to realize that Jesus actually acted like God in human form. They realized that Jesus did the things that, in the Old Testament, God's Holy Spirit had done. It was by thinking about Jesus that they came to understand that he was one with the Spirit and the Father.

The resulting concept is difficult to understand intellectually, but if we try to put ourselves into the shoes of the first Christians, we will see that this explanation about God's character fits best with the other things we know about God.

Despite the difficulties, the Trinity is the best way of understanding God. Furthermore, this understanding is not just a head game. This truth about God is practical. It really does help the other pieces of the puzzle fit into place. Understanding more of the Holy Trinity helps us to understand God better; and more important, it helps us experience God better.

God Talk

Since God is ultimately beyond our comprehension it is appropriate to use a mysterious concept to indicate what he is like.

The Trinity itself is a mystery — that is to say, it is a truth we can experience, even if we cannot fully explain it. That might sound a little suspicious, but when you think about it there is another, very ordinary aspect of life where this is also true. Love is something we can experience but in the end not fully explain. The Trinity is like that, too.

The mystery of the Trinity has been explained with many types of picture language. St. Patrick said it was like a clover leaf — one leaf, but three leaves. Others have said it is like water; it takes three forms — solid, liquid, and gas — but all three are still water. All of these descriptions might help people understand the Trinity, but none of them are totally satisfactory. They can never be more than picture language to try to explain what is beyond our ability to understand.

One of the reasons none of these word pictures works completely is because all of them are just pictures. If God is Three in One, we can't make a picture of him. This is because God the Three in One is as much about what God *does* as what he is.

We call the Father, Son, and Holy Spirit *persons* because, like any person, they each have distinct characteristics and ways of acting.

The Family God

That is why the best way to speak of the Holy Trinity is to talk about family life. God's life is not empty and dead. Instead it is a dynamic loving relationship among three persons. The Father, the Son, and the Holy Spirit are like a human family. A man, woman, and child are united as one through the love in a marriage, and that three-way union of love reflects the nature of God himself.

If God is like a family, then at the core of God's life is love. This is the practical and astounding truth that is unlocked by the mystery of the Holy Trinity: that God is love. If God is love, then we come to know God by learning more about love. We also experience the reality of the Trinity by experiencing the reality of God's love in our lives.

We learn best about love by being members of a family. That is why when we become Christians it is said that we are being "adopted" as God's children. This not only means that we enter the family of all other people who believe, but we enter the "family" that is made up of Father, Son, and Holy Spirit.

Welcome Home

This is what Jesus came to accomplish. He broke down the barrier between God and humanity to welcome us into a relationship with his own Father, God. Like an older brother, Jesus came into this world to seek and to save his lost brothers and sisters and bring them home.

We claim our family inheritance by realizing we are cut off from God, deciding to switch sides, and being baptized. Baptism is a ritual that brings about the truth it signifies. Being put into the water at Baptism is a sign of being put into Christ's death. Rising up out of the water is a sign of rising up with Christ in his resurrection. In other words, through Baptism we are being "put into" Christ. We become one with Christ, and he becomes one with us.

When Jesus was baptized the voice from heaven said, "This is my beloved Son"[36] and the Holy Spirit descended like a dove. This was a picture that in Baptism Father, Son, and Holy Spirit are together as one, powerful, dynamic unit.

Therefore, when you become a Christian you are baptized not just in the name of Christ, but in the name of the Father, the Son,

[36]Matthew 3:17.

and the Holy Spirit. This is because through Baptism we really do enter into a relationship with the God who is Father, Son, and Holy Spirit.

Just as the Father said to Jesus, "You are my beloved Son," so at our Baptism into Jesus Christ God says to us, "You are my beloved child." Through this transaction we become part of God's family. God becomes our Father, Jesus becomes our Brother, and the Holy Spirit enters our life to bring us right into the center of that reality that is God himself.

Christ's Life Within Us

If you have stayed with me thus far you will see that the Christian faith is not simply about obeying a set of religious rules or just trying hard to be a good person. Christianity is far more radical than that. The Christian faith is about accepting God into the very core of our lives. When we are baptized, the life force of Jesus Christ enters our life and begins a transformation within us.

Father, Son, and Holy Spirit exist in perfect unity. As Christ enters into our life he wants to create a new unity with us. Jesus prayed that his followers might be one as he and the Father are one. Jesus was one with the Father in what he was — like the Father, fully divine — but also in what he *did*. That's the oneness that we are to imitate. All the chaotic, divided parts of us are to be harmonized and work together in unity. Our body, our mind, and our spirit are meant to work as one — not be divided against each other. Likewise we should work in harmony with other people, united in a common purpose of truth and love.

It is important to get a glimpse of what the Holy Trinity means, because then we come to realize the simple truth that as we accept Christ into our lives we are actually opening the very heart of our being to God himself. The three-way God of love is working in us and through us to bring us to our final destiny. That destiny is nothing less than a life lived within the everlasting power and glory of God's own life of love.

Love Binds Them All Together

Just as it is impossible to explain love fully, it is impossible to explain the Trinity fully (although wise theologians over the centuries have surely helped advance our understanding). But just as it is possible to know love by experiencing it, so it is possible to begin to understand the Trinity by experiencing God's powerful love.

By *love* I don't mean the sentimental stuff of romantic movies and love songs. These are fine, but I am talking about something far greater, and far more mysterious and noble and tragic and true. The love I am talking about really *is* the "force" that binds all things together.

The force that moves the sun and the other stars is the power of love. Love is the outgoing goodness of God in the universe. Love is also the power that binds the three persons of the Trinity together. Love attracts the Father, the Son, and the Holy Spirit and binds them in a perfect harmony and unity like a great magnetic force.

This is the powerful love that we are called to share in. Love binds us together with one another, but it is also binds us into the very heart of the Trinity. We tap into that love and become a part of it as you might plug into an electric circuit.

All You Need Is Love

To be a Christian, therefore, means learning to live and move within and through the power of love. The New Testament says, "Those who live in love live in God, and God lives in them."[37]

[37]Cf. 1 John 4:16.

As we live a life of love for ourselves, for our families, for other people, and for the world we are not just making the world a better, nicer place, but we are also joining ourselves with the heart of God.

The love of God is the energy force that draws us into relationship with him, but all of our lesser loves on earth are also part of that greater love. When we live in the love of a human family, when we engage in loving actions toward others, when we forgive and make time for others, we do so within the greater love that binds God together, and which moves the sun and the stars.

Jesus Christ is the way for us to be bound into this wonderful energy supply called love. He shows us that love in its fullness and empowers us to live within that love more and more each day. Do you want to have a full and abundant life and make the world a better place? Do you want to find true love in this life, and a love that will last forever? Do you want to discover the secret of true happiness? Do you want to live life to the full and take hold of all that life has to offer?

Then open your life to this power of love. It is available to all. It is not easy to claim it, for everything within us whispers that we should turn away from this love. But if we give ourselves to this love and ask for the gift of this love, then it will most certainly be given and we will be able to begin the greatest adventure that life has to offer.

Down through the ages, real, ordinary people have been transformed by the power of God's love in their lives. They have given themselves totally to this love, and it has burned in their lives with such radiance and power that the whole world has seen their lives transformed.

How this amazing transformation can happen is the subject of the next section.

Christianity Pure and Simple

GOING WITH GOD

Connecting with the Power Source

For some time I have been talking about the power of transformation in our lives, and where that power comes from. I've done this because it is important to realize that we cannot change ourselves. Bookstores are full of self-help books. These books contain much that is good and helpful, but there is a basic flaw in all of them. They don't put you in touch with a power greater than yourself.

Christians believe that God's Holy Spirit gives us an amazing power source for change in our lives. Because of Jesus Christ's death and resurrection, that power source is available to every person who asks for it. This burning energy source is necessary if we really want to change for good.

It's not hard to connect with this fire force, but the first and most important step is to realize that we *need* this power of change in our lives, and that we cannot change on our own.

Turning Around

One reason self-help books sell so well is that we all want to believe that we can change without the help of God. I'm sorry. We can't. We just don't have the power to change permanently on our own. Of course we can make improvements to our lives, but we cannot change the way we really are deep down inside.

There is only one power that can bring that kind of inner revolution, and that is the spiritual power unleashed by the Holy Spirit. The first step toward receiving this power is to realize that we need it. This means we have to change our mind. We have to see, first of all, that we cannot change ourselves by ourselves. This means we have to experience a fundamental shift in our attitude.

We do not need just an ordinary type of changed mind. Instead we need a radical realignment of our whole life. We need to see that we are headed in the wrong direction and resolve to change course entirely.

Realizing that we are on the wrong course is not the same thing as saying we are totally and utterly wrong in everything. It just means we have been building on sand when we should have been building on solid rock. It means we begin to say, "I need help."

Come Down, O Love Divine

Really admitting that we need help doesn't come easily. The conviction that we really are all right as we are dies hard. Sometimes we come to a true reversal of our attitude only because we have reached rock bottom in life. Through illness, bereavement, bad luck, or our own stupid choices we come to the point where we have nowhere else to turn, and we realize then at the very deepest level of our personalities that we need help and only God can bail us out.

This ground-level change of heart is not just admitting that in theory we need help, but *knowing* that we need help. Then we can really turn to God and ask for the Holy Spirit to come to our aid. At that point we are open to receive the gift of Divine Love or the gift of the Holy Spirit in a new way.

If we are not at rock bottom, but we still want to understand what this kind of change of heart is about, it is enough to ask for the gift of repentance. *Repentance* is a technical word for this ground-level shift of awareness. Then the Holy Spirit will help us to understand our deepest need in a more powerful way. Once we have realized our need, we will be ready to receive the power to change.

Jesus Christ released that power in the world. All we need to do is acknowledge that fact and ask for his Spirit within our lives. He has promised to send that Spirit, and if we ask, we will most certainly receive. If we seek, he has promised that we will find the treasure. Trusting that he will give us the power to change is called *faith*.

Teamwork Required

Having repentance and faith is not a once-and-done thing. It is true that we need to come to a set time when we really do turn toward God for good, but we also need to check our spiritual compass daily. Day by day, throughout our lives, we need to check whether we are aware of our need for God and whether we are living in faith.

Living this way is an adventure. It means new possibilities open up, because God is in charge now, not we. Those who live by faith are on a journey into a new and unknown land — a land that promises to be full of new riches as well as new challenges.

Living in repentance and faith opens us up to God's marvelous way of working in the world. Suddenly we can see that someone else is working in and through our lives to transform us into all that we can be. Furthermore, he is working through us to change the world. We realize we have become his agents in the world, and that if we stay with him, fantastic and wonderful things can happen.

To stay in this state of repentance and faith, we must work with the Holy Spirit. The help that God gives us, first to understand him and then to turn toward him regularly, is called *grace*. Living in a "state of grace" means that we dwell constantly in an awareness that we need God and that he is always by our side.

The Great Challenge

God helps us to see our need and to turn toward him, but we must always remember that God will not override our will. He will not force us to love him. If he did, the result would not be love. For love to be real, we must choose to turn from our own way and follow God's way.

God gives us the power to choose, and the specific power to choose him and his love, but we must use that power. God's help is available to everyone. All we need to do is ask, and the Holy Spirit will help us. We then have to act within that power in order to be transformed

The work of total transformation is not easy or quick. In fact, you will find that trying to follow God's way is the hardest thing you have ever done. Those of us who are trying to follow this path admit that we often get confused and lose our way. Many times we stumble and fall on the path to perfection. What matters is not how often we fall, but how often we get up.

The sign that the Holy Spirit is at work in our lives is that we can see new powers developing in our lives. A new order grows within us; certain abilities that were lying dormant suddenly start to develop; in many practical ways our lives begin to change. The Spirit gives these new powers to help us to grow as people and to understand God's ways and wisdom better.

The Gifts of the Holy Spirit

The gifts of the Holy Spirit are supernatural. They are qualities of mind, intelligence, and spirit that help us to grow into all that God created us to be. Yet although they are supernatural gifts, they are expressed and worked out in our lives in seemingly natural ways.

The Holy Spirit gives a whole range of new abilities, but there are seven recognized gifts that we can notice becoming active in people's lives.

The first of the seven gifts of the Holy Spirit is *wisdom*. Wisdom was the power of God that helped to make all things. Wisdom helps us to see clearly; to get our priorities right and grow in understanding.

Understanding is the second gift of the Holy Spirit. It is not easy to understand spiritual matters. Our eyes are darkened by sin, but the Holy Spirit has been given to teach us all things. As we learn more about our faith the Holy Spirit is there as our teacher and mentor. With the gift of understanding, our range of interests changes. We discover that we are more and more interested in spiritual things.

It is difficult to know the right way through life. We are often faced with difficult decisions. As we learn to listen to the Holy Spirit in our lives these decisions become easier. We are able to see the right way and discern what is best. The ability to discern what is right and wrong and to understand which spiritual things are true and false is called *counsel* and is the third gift of the Spirit.

The fourth gift is *fortitude*. This is the supernatural strength to do what is right. When we are faced with a temptation, if we ask the Holy Spirit for help, it will be there. In practical terms fortitude helps us to stand up for what is right.

Knowledge is another gift of the Holy Spirit. This is not just head knowledge, but a real experience of spiritual truths. This kind of knowledge of life is the kind you have when you're in love, not the kind you get from reading love poems. The spiritual gift of knowledge is not purely intellectual. It is practical and useful. With this kind of knowledge we can help others to know the truth and live by it.

Piety is the gift to live the spiritual life in all naturalness and goodness. It is not about trying hard to be holy and good, but the supernatural ability to be holy and good with joy and ease. A truly pious person does try hard to be good, but eventually the Spirit brings him to a point at which he does good as part of his nature.

This is like an athlete who trains hard, but then wins the race with ease and a sense of exhilaration.

The last gift is *fear of the Lord*. This does not mean that we tremble in constant anxiety in the face of God. Instead it means that we live in a state of repentance and faith. Fear of the Lord is a constant joyful awareness that we need God and that he is with us always.

TOTAL TRANSFORMATION

Signs of Life

When the Holy Spirit begins to work in our life, it is as if we become a new person. The old things have passed away, and all things have become new. We see not only ourselves but everyone in a new light. Indeed, we see the whole world in a new way.

As we live in the Spirit, other people will begin to see that there is something different about us. Perhaps they won't be able define it, but they will realize that our priorities have changed. The Holy Spirit has given us a new way of seeing, and a new way of being.

Of course, the new person is not made perfect immediately. We have to work hard with God for the Holy Spirit to take control of our lives. But eventually we find that our old habits are replaced by new ways of thinking and behaving. Bit by bit in our daily lives we find that change is taking place. We really *are* becoming more patient with our children, with our difficult family members, or with that awkward person at work.

The Spirit works within our ordinary lives to give them an extraordinary wealth of meaning, purpose, and power. This process of perfection is gradual and natural. Like the growth of a great tree, it takes time for the roots to go deep. It takes time for the branches to grow and for the fruit to ripen, but when the fruit is ripe everyone benefits.

Likewise, the Spirit brings to fruition certain recognizable traits within the spiritual person. These characteristics are called the fruits of the Holy Spirit. The fruits of the Holy Spirit are developed by the supernatural work of the Spirit. Although the Spirit is supernatural, his work is not unnatural. The fruits of the Spirit are the best of our human character brought to full development by the Spirit's power.

The Fruits of Life

The first fruit is *charity*. Now, charity is not just giving money to an organization that helps poor people. Neither is charity simply doing good to others. Instead it is an inner quality — the perfection of love in which we see and love others as they are. In our daily lives charity makes us naturally more patient and tolerant because deep down we really have come to desire the best for others — not just for ourselves.

Joy is the second fruit that the Spirit helps to ripen in our lives. Joy is not just happiness or fun. Instead Christian joy is a supernatural kind of happiness. Joy is marked by a special spiritual energy and enthusiasm for life. The Spirit brings joy because the person can see that an all-loving God is at work in the world. Because of this he really can see the positive side of every problem.

Joy is linked with the third fruit: *peace*. The Bible talks about "the peace that passes all understanding,"[38] and Jesus said to his disciples, "I give you peace. Not peace as the world gives."[39] The person who lives in the power of the Holy Spirit knows a deep

[38]Cf. Philippians 4:7.
[39]Cf. John 14:27.

peace even when things go wrong. The Spirit-filled person has peace because he knows that God is in charge, and in the end all shall be well.

Along with inner peace and charity come *patience* and *kindness*. For a Christian, patience and kindness are not simply a matter of being polite and having good manners. Instead the person who is filled with the Holy Spirit is patient and kind not because he's trying to be, but because genuine patience and kindness have become part of his nature.

It is the same thing with the other fruits of the Spirit. A person is good, generous, gentle, faithful, and modest, not so much because he is trying hard to be that way, but because his nature has been transformed, and he has become all that he was first created to be.

Becoming Sons and Daughters of God

We all share the same destiny as Jesus: to be all that we were created to be. We are all meant to become the sons and daughters of God; the brothers and sisters of Christ. Over and over again throughout the writings of the New Testament, and in the lives and writings of all the Christian saints, we are called not to a life of religious rules and regulations, but a life that is transformed by the power of God.

Religion has become irrelevant and meaningless to many people because of this fundamental mistake. They have misunderstood the most important thing. Jesus did not come to enforce a great list of rules. The Christian faith is not first and foremost a religion of respectability and good manners. It is a religion that fills, transforms, and glorifies individual human beings.

Of course, this is not easy, but Thérèse of Lisieux calls us to the challenge with youthful zeal: "You cannot be half a saint," she cries. "You must be a whole saint or no saint at all!" A saint is not simply a pious goody-goody. The saints are brave, idealistic, unyielding, and devoted heroes. They are the spiritual equivalents of world-champion mountain climbers. The saints are utterly committed to their beliefs. They love God with all the heart, mind, and strength.

In doing so, they show us the possibility of total transformation into radiant and powerful people. This is what Christianity is about: no less than the total transformation of our lives into all that we were created to be — and what we are created to be are sons and daughters of the living God.

Change the World (and Start with Yourself)

As this conversion takes place in our lives, it is also happening in the lives of millions of other people all over the world. The work of the Holy Spirit down through the ages is to convert not just individuals to the will of God, but to bring the whole world back into relationship with him.

Do you want to change the world? Change yourself first, by opening yourself up to the power of the Person who made you. As the Holy Spirit transforms our lives we begin to fit into God's plan for the whole world. We become part of a worldwide movement that is changing the course of history.

The study of history shows that it is the religious ideas of individuals and nations that motivate the transformation of history. Believers transform the world. Unbelievers cannot even transform themselves. As we believe, so we will do, and if we believe, the Holy Spirit will transform our lives so we can be part of his action in the world.

There is a group of people who will have given themselves to this very action. This international group of believers are all empowered by the Holy Spirit. All of them are all working together with the spirit as much as they can. Before Jesus left this earth he not only gave his Holy Spirit to his followers, but he also told his followers to form a community of all those who were filled with his Holy Spirit. This little group of Holy Spirit people has grown for the last two thousand years, filling every corner of the world. This group of people is called the Church.

THE PEOPLE OF GOD

As It Was in the Beginning

From the very beginning God began his work on earth within a family. The Jewish writers were keen to show that they had descended from their father Abraham, and that he had descended from Adam and Eve. In other words, the special relationship that God had established with Adam and Eve continued down through the generations.

The Old Testament is the story not just of Spirit-filled individuals like Abraham, Moses, Joshua, David, and the prophets. It is also the story of a Spirit-filled people we call the Jews. Throughout the Old Testament God is concerned with the whole family of Abraham — not just with certain individuals.

This shows God's way of working in the world. He works through a chosen group of people. God's Spirit fills the individuals in that family, but the Spirit also directs the whole people of God. God works in the world both through individuals and through a whole body of faithful people.

The Church Is the Family of Christ

The same Holy Spirit who filled, renewed, guided, and taught the Old Testament people of God was given to the followers of

Jesus at Pentecost. In this, a new kind of spiritual family was established. Because each individual has a share in the same Spirit, there is a family bond between them. Jesus said that each one is his brother or sister. He said, "The one who does the will of my Father is my brother or my sister."[40]

If those who receive the Holy Spirit are brothers and sisters of Jesus, they are also brothers and sisters of each other. Because they share in the same spirit they are members of the same family. This is not just a symbol or a way of speaking. This is a reality. Through the Holy Spirit every other Christian really is my spiritual brother or sister.

The Church, therefore, is not just a collection of like-minded people. A political party, a sports team, an academic society — all of these are simply organizations of people with certain shared goals and interests. The Church, on the other hand, is more than that. It is a family. All who belong to it are members of the great family of God.

The Church Is the Body of Christ

The Church is a family, but the New Testament uses another image to talk about the people of God. It says that the Church is the "the Body of Christ."[41] Each member of the Church is like a cell in the Body. As such, every member is dependent on every other member. They cannot exist on their own.

Once again, this is not simply a poetic way of speaking. In a very real sense the Church is Christ's Body alive here on earth today. The body of all people who believe in Christ do his work in the world.

[40]Cf. Matthew 12:50.
[41]1 Corinthians 12:27.

Those who are alive in the Spirit are alive to one another. The Spirit is constantly at work keeping all the Spirit-filled people working together in harmony like members of a vast orchestra. In this way, all the individual Christians do what they can do best, but at the same time they are working together with one another to accomplish Christ's plan of world transformation.

If the Church is the Body of Christ, we would expect the Church to show Christ at work in the world today. This is exactly what we do find. In earlier chapters we saw how the Spirit brings new life, freedom, and understanding. Then we saw that Jesus did that same work when he was on earth. Now he does this work through the ministry of the Spirit-filled people of God.

The Body of Christ Brings New Life
One of the things the Holy Spirit does is to bring new life. The Holy Spirit was there at the beginning of creation, bringing life out of the dark watery chaos.

Jesus breathed new life into his followers after his resurrection, and he linked this new life with the symbol of water: "You must be born again of water and the spirit." I will discuss this more later, but here it is enough to say that through the Church we receive the gift of Baptism. By cleansing us with water God brings us into a new kind of spiritual life. We receive the gift of the Spirit, but we do so through the ministry of God's people on earth: the Church.

The Church is at work in the world, bringing about new life in all sorts of ways. Through education, healing ministries, health care, political involvement, pastoral care, and spiritual teaching, Christ's Body, the Church, continues to do his work of bringing new life to a dark, chaotic world.

In our individual lives we find real healing within the family of the Church as well. All of us have dark areas of our lives that need the light of Christ. Whether they are evil things we've done or evil things that have been done to us, these wounds can be healed by the power of the Holy Spirit at work in the Church.

If we have committed ourselves to live in the Spirit, we have our work cut out for us. It is part of our mission first to experience God's healing and wholeness, then to bring that new life to others, so that the whole world can be renewed with God's life.

The Body of Christ Brings Freedom

The Holy Spirit brought freedom. Jesus brought freedom. The Church does the same work. Through forgiveness Jesus set people free to live a new kind of life, and in the Gospels Jesus gave his Apostles authority to forgive sins in his name. He said, "As the Father has sent me, so I am sending you."[42] This authority to forgive sins was passed down from the first Apostles to the Church leaders who came after them and can still be found in the Church today.

The Church is busy bringing the freedom of Jesus to the world in all sorts of other ways: through charity, counseling, and pro-life work; by speaking out against oppression, immorality, and injustice in the political arena; by reaching out to the marginalized in society. The Spirit, therefore, is not just our private gift. The Spirit should lead each one of us to work with our brothers and sisters to bring freedom, justice, and peace to everyone.

The Church Teaches with Power

In the Old Testament the Holy Spirit taught the people the truth about God. Jesus *was* the truth about God, and his Body on earth (the Church) continues the essential work of teaching people the truth.

[42] Cf. John 20:21.

When Jesus was on earth the people were amazed because he taught the truth with authority. Before he went back to heaven, Jesus shared with his Apostles his authority to know and teach the truth. He said, "All authority on heaven and on earth has been given to me. Go, therefore, and teach all nations, baptizing them in the name of the Father, the Son, and the Holy Spirit."[43]

In other words, as well as telling his Apostles to go out into the world and preach the gospel, Jesus was also giving them the *authority* to do so. This is very important for us today. There are many religious teachers in the world. How do we know which ones truly speak from God?

I will say more about this later, but here it is enough to say that, through the power of the Holy Spirit, the Church down through the ages has continued to teach the truth with the same authority of Jesus. If we want to understand the truth about God most fully, then we look to Christ, and the Body of Christ here on earth is the community of Spirit-filled people he established.

The Body of Christ helps us to understand the truth about God, and the Spirit that fills the Church helps us share that truth with others. If we are Spirit-filled people, this is part of our way of working with the Spirit of Christ in the world.

Getting Ready for the Great Battle

Once we have accepted the Holy Spirit into our lives, we have not reached the end of the journey; we have only just started. The Christian life is an exciting journey. It is a pilgrimage to a glorious destination. It's also a challenge; but luckily we do not travel alone. In fact, it is impossible for us to travel this journey alone. By the simple fact that we are all joined to the same Body of Christ,

[43]Cf. Matthew 28:18-19.

we are invisibly connected with everyone else who is traveling the same path.

It's a good thing we do not travel alone, because the journey is difficult. There are many hardships along the way; there are enemies who wish to attack us. We struggle against the dark side of our nature and against the dark forces arrayed against us.

The next section of this book tells you how to join in the battle. It tells you where to find help. It tells you how God enables you to fight the battle. And it tells you how, through the power of the Holy Spirit, you can fight the good fight, finish the course, and lay hold of the great prize that has been prepared for you.

Chapter Four

The Great Battle

SOLDIERS OF CHRIST

Time and again a favorite story of mine has been voted the best book of the twentieth century: J.R.R. Tolkien's *The Lord of the Rings*.

Not everybody is a fan of fantasy stories, and some people just aren't interested in the adventures of a furry-footed hobbit named Frodo. However, the huge popularity of Tolkien's book and the blockbuster success of the films adapted from it indicate that there is something in the story that keeps people coming back for more.

At the very heart of *The Lord of the Rings* and every other classic tale is the battle of good against evil. You may not be a fan of *The Lord of the Rings*, but whatever kind of story or film you like, some kind of conflict likely lies at the heart of the story. The villain may not be supremely evil. Indeed, the thing to be overcome might be the hero's circumstances, disability, or personal problem. But whatever it is, there is some evil to be conquered if the good person is going to survive and thrive.

We are captivated by great stories in which the hero fights against evil, because deep down we are all aware of some evil in our lives. Evil threatens us from the world around us, but it also threatens us from within. We have a deep instinct that, unless we are engaged in the battle against that evil, we can be quickly swallowed up by it.

Common Sense and the Existence of Evil

Of course, some people think that there's no such thing as good and evil, not *really*. They say that what we call "good" is simply what seems good for us and what we call "evil" is what we think is bad for us. They say that to live together peacefully, we need to agree on some basic rights and wrongs; thus good and evil are just useful terms that help to oil the wheels of society. Can this be so?

It is strange that anyone could hold an opinion like this at the beginning of the twenty-first century. After all, in the last century we have seen some of the most unimaginable evil the world has ever experienced. More people have been unjustly imprisoned, tortured, mutilated, and slaughtered than ever before. Can we face the horrors of Auschwitz, the Rwanda massacres, or the 9/11 attacks and shrug our shoulders and say, "These things only *seemed* evil to the people who died that day"?

This simply won't do. If we have any morsel of humanity within us, we must conclude that these, and many other instances, are examples of real evil. To fail to call these things evil is not simply to have a different opinion, but to be just plain wrong.

To be honest, we *have* to admit that this evil is at work in the world right now. In fact, one of the reasons this evil has grown is because the people who committed it didn't think it was evil. The Nazis thought the elimination of the Jews was a good and necessary act of ethnic cleansing. The very denial of the reality of good and evil allows the most terrible evils to flourish.

Furthermore, if we are really honest, we will admit that there is a shadow side in all of us, one that could lead each one of us to commit horrific crimes if the circumstances were right.

We tell ourselves that we would never take part in mass murder, the torture of innocent people, or the rape and mutilation of defenseless children. But in the context of war and hardship we see that very ordinary people do, in fact, both tolerate and commit very horrific crimes — crimes of which they never thought they would be capable.

We Cannot Be Neutral

The capability of terrible evil is present in every human heart, and for some it takes only the right circumstances to bring that beast to the surface. Of course, you might want to imagine that the beast is safely chained up in *your* dark places and that you would never do anything terribly wrong. That is what I would like to believe about myself.

But I'm not so sure that my dark side is totally under control. Are you sure yours is? When I lose my temper, when I give in to lust or greed and indulge myself, that beast soon starts showing its teeth. I start to become less patient and more violent toward those I live with. Furthermore, my own selfishness not only causes me to do bad things; it also keeps me from doing good things. The things I want to do, I can't; and the things I don't want to do, I do.

The fact of the matter is that each one of us is locked into this battle of good and evil every day of our lives, whether we like it or not. Because our human nature is selfish we are in conflict with other people whose natures are also selfish. Conflict lies at the heart of our daily existence.

We might wish to opt out of the conflict, but that is impossible, too. If there really is a terrible evil out there, then, if we are good we must fight against it. There are only two choices: fight against the evil or give in to the evil.

Usually the Battle Is Clear

It is easy to make this battle more complicated than it actually is. We can pretend that the battle is difficult to understand. We can say that "things are never so black and white" or "it is never clear what is right and wrong."

It's true that some moral choices are difficult and nuanced. But most are not. Most of the time moral choices are very clear and simple. Living by those choices might not be easy, but seeing the choice itself is easy. In most situations most people know what is right and what is wrong. Usually the confusion comes in when they decide they want to do something wrong. Suddenly we imagine that morality is awfully difficult and complex, when all we are really doing is trying to justify our decision to break the rules.

Religion gives us rules to live by, but society does, too. The basic rules are universal to all human beings. The details might vary from one society to another, but the essential guidelines can be put quite simply: it is good to live for others and selfish to live only for ourselves. Being untruthful is wrong; telling the truth is right. Hurting others is wrong; helping others is right. Stealing is wrong; giving is right. Betraying loved ones is wrong; being loyal is right.

In most situations, therefore, recognizing the choice between right and wrong is easy. We might not have the courage and confidence to *do* what is right, but that is a different matter. Yet if we can see what is right and wrong, it is up to us to try our best to do the right thing and so help in the battle against evil.

You Can Make a Difference

We would like to imagine that our own lives aren't really part of the great battle. We wish to be left on our own. We want to mind our own business. We don't think our own little lives are particularly selfish, and we don't see why our personal choices should make much difference.

When faced with this complacency in my own life, I try to turn around and ask myself why I should be exempt from the battle.

Can I really stand by and do nothing? If there is a great struggle between good and evil, can I just hope for a quiet life and hope to avoid the conflict? What sort of a life is that? If I do not join in the battle, I will have wasted my life in easy comfort.

Instead of doing nothing, I should be using the life that has been given to me to make the world a better place. Each of us wants life to have a purpose and meaning. The greatest purpose is the fight against evil. Do we think we are too small to make a difference? The world has always been changed by individuals, not by committees. There is a great and eternal destiny for each one of us if we will only join the battle.

You Do Not Fight Alone

The encouraging thing in this battle is that we do not fight alone. Every other human being is also engaged in the fight. In the midst of our ordinary, mundane lives we may not see the reality of this, but it is true: every person you meet is fighting the shadows or giving in to the shadows a little bit more every day.

Terrible situations in war and extreme social conditions show that the vast majority of human beings actually want to fight on the right side. No matter what their religion or belief system, most people understand the basic decent thing to do. Most people want to stand up for the right when they have the chance.

As a result, when you decide to enter the battle actively, you will find that you are fighting alongside a whole host of other people. Human beings from every nation, and from every religion and from every class of life will be there on your side, fighting for honesty, justice, peace, prosperity, and goodness.

They do not fight only in the realm of ideas and great projects. The real battle goes on in the nitty-gritty of everyday life. Those who are engaged in the battle know that the front line is in the home, the workplace, the schools, and the community where they live. The war is huge, but every soldier contributes in his own humble and mundane way.

Christians believe that joining in this fight against evil is at the very heart of their own religious commitment. When people are baptized, they do not merely affirm their belief that Jesus Christ is the Son of God, and that he died for them; they do not just sit back and wait to coast along to heaven when they die. Instead the Christian commitment is a commitment to take up arms.

Christians commit themselves to the battle for life. As they do, they join an army of others within their own community, around the world, and throughout the ages who have also seen where the battle lines are and joined in to fight the good fight.

THE ARMIES OF DARKNESS AND LIGHT

Two Levels of Battle

Whenever we watch the news or read a paper we are confronted with the reality of the fight between good and evil. This is the physical, historical dimension to the battle between good and evil: war, crime, conflict, injustice.

But the battle is going on at a deeper level at the same time. At this level the struggle is spiritual and moral — not just physical and historical.

Because we human beings are both physical and spiritual it is possible for us to join in the battle in two ways. We can fight on the side of goodness and light through our physical actions by doing good in the world, and we can also join in the spiritual battle against the forces of evil.

Christianity is a practical religion. It works. It helps us to fight the battle against evil on both levels at the same time. An active

Christian does not simply pray about the troubles in the world and then do nothing. Neither does he simply work hard to make the world a better place. Instead the active Christian prays hard and works hard. He uses both physical weapons and spiritual weapons in the battle against evil.

The Enemy Is Real

God and the Devil. Good and evil. Darkness and light. This is not just fantasy language or a symbolic way of looking at the world. The battle is real. Evil is real. Furthermore, that evil is planned and accomplished by real personalities. This is true on both the physical and spiritual levels.

When we consider the crimes committed by Hitler, Stalin, or Osama bin Laden; when we consider the crimes of a serial rapist or a sadistic child killer, we know that there are some people who have given themselves to evil. These human beings are the physical perpetrators of evil.

There are spiritual agents of evil as well. Down through ages, in every society there is evidence of malignant forces — evil personalities who are spiritual and totally twisted by evil. Christians believe there are creatures who exist in a purely spiritual dimension. The good ones are called angels, and the ones who have fallen into evil are called demons.

These evil spirits infest the world. They tempt people to commit crimes. If invited in, they can take over people's personalities and commit terrible atrocities through them. There is plenty of evidence from all over the world to show that these evil spirits really do exist and can really influence individual lives and world events.

As a result, when we enter the battle against evil we will be opposed by evil spiritual forces as well as by evil human beings. We fight against the two different forces with different weapons. We use physical means to fight the physical battle, but we must use spiritual means to combat spiritual enemies.

Secret Allies

Sometimes it might look as if the forces of evil are winning, but those who fight within the Christian Church are fighting on the side that has already won. When Jesus Christ rose from the dead, death and evil were defeated. The war has not yet been completed, but the seed of evil's defeat has been planted.

When Jesus Christ founded the Church he said, "The gates of hell will never be able to prevail against it."[44] In other words, those who follow Christ might lose some battles, but they cannot lose the war. As a result, when we become Christians and join the Church, we join a company of triumphant warriors.

In this battle the Christian has three types of secret allies with which the forces of darkness have not reckoned. First, when a person becomes a Christian he immediately joins a whole range of fellow fighters across the world. All those who follow Christ become his brothers and sisters. They also become his fellow foot soldiers. Like him, they are committed to the battle and fight by his side.

A Christian is also joined by the vast multitude of Christians who have left this physical life, but still live in the spiritual realm. All those who have died in the faith of Christ still live in his victory. They are still interested and involved in the battles going on here on earth. When Christians love and pray to those people, called the saints, they are enlisting their help for the ongoing battle.

[44]Cf. Matthew 16:18.

Those who fight for what is right also have the help of the spiritual powers who are on the side of goodness and light. Angels are God's messengers. They are also our helpers. In the spiritual battle, they are committed to strengthening, guiding, and protecting us.

We do not fight alone. The angels and our fellow Christians — both alive and dead in Christ — fight by our side.

Physical Weapons, Spiritual Battlegrounds

Our bodies are our physical weapons in the battle. The New Testament says our bodies "are the temple of the Holy Spirit."[45] In other words, our bodies are the special dwelling place of the Holy Spirit, and it is through our bodies that the Holy Spirit of Christ can conduct his battles against evil.

Our hands, therefore, can become the hands of Christ in the world. Our lips can speak his words, and our feet can run to do his will. With our bodies we live and move in the physical realm, and with our bodies we fight in the spiritual battle. When we help the sick, feed the hungry, or visit the imprisoned, we are using our bodies to fight evil.

Our bodies are not simply shells for our souls. Our soul does not inhabit a body as a person sits inside a car. Instead our bodies and souls are united in a single being. Our souls reside in our bodies more as water in a sponge than as water in a cup. Because of this, our spiritual health and our physical health are interlinked.

What we do with our bodies, therefore, can affect the state of our souls; and likewise, what we do with our souls can affect the state of our bodies. It will be difficult to pray and worship, for instance, if our bodies are addicted to the poison of bad food, bad drugs, alcohol, or tobacco smoke. It will also be impossible to pray

[45]Cf. 1 Corinthians 6:19.

and worship if our minds are full of hatred and vengeful thoughts, envy, pornographic images, greedy ambitions, fear, and pride.

Likewise, what we do with our souls impacts our bodies and minds. If we pray, if we submit to God's way, if we ask the Holy Spirit to fill our lives and guide us, we will benefit physically and mentally. Many studies have shown that people who pray and meditate enjoy better health, have better marriages, heal faster, and are more optimistic about the future.

Spiritual Weapons

It is easy to forget that there is also a spiritual dimension to the battle against evil. It is easy to imagine that we can do nothing worthwhile in the spiritual realm. This is not so. We can have great spiritual power and use that power for good.

The way to develop that spiritual power is to ask to be filled with the Holy Spirit. The Holy Spirit enables us to understand the rules of battle. The Spirit helps us discern the best way to fight and where to focus our energy. The Spirit also gives us the spiritual energy to take up the fight.

We stay tuned in to the Spirit through prayer, meditation, contemplation, and worship. Prayer is focused spiritual energy. Prayer is a way to align our will with God's will in order to accomplish great things in the spiritual realm. I will say more about prayer later, but it is enough at this point to say that there are many forms of prayer, and each person needs to find which works best.

THE MOST POWERFUL WEAPONS OF ALL

The Physical/Spiritual Weapons

Because we are both spiritual and physical creatures we fight the battle against evil in both spiritual and physical ways. Physical actions against evil are the good deeds we do. Spiritual actions are prayer, meditation, and worship.

But it is artificial to separate the spiritual from the physical. Within us the spiritual and physical dimensions are totally one. Our physical actions have spiritual meaning, and our prayers involve our bodies. One of the results of God's taking human form in Jesus Christ is that the barrier between the spiritual and physical realms was broken forever.

In Jesus the spiritual and the physical are perfectly united. If we are to become more like Jesus, we should move closer to that same unity between the physical and spiritual realms. This is part of the battle against evil. Those who are given to evil are deeply divided within, and their spiritual and physical natures are at war. Those who are moving toward goodness are also moving toward wholeness and inner unity. When we pursue the good, we are also working to unify our spiritual and physical dimensions.

To bring us into this unity Christians have been given special weapons for the battle that combine the spiritual and the physical in one action. These weapons are called *sacraments*. The word *sacrament* means "mystery" but is also related to the word *covenant*. A covenant is a solemn promise between two parties that is sealed by a physical action. So, for example, a marriage covenant is sealed with rings, or a peace treaty might be sealed with a ceremony in which swords are exchanged, then solemnly broken.

In a sacrament, we participate in a solemn ceremony that is both physical and spiritual. The physical aspect of the sacrament makes real what it symbolizes spiritually. For example, when two people make love, that physical action seals their marriage and a physical/spiritual bond is actually established between them.

The same is true of all the sacraments. They are formal, solemn ceremonies in which a physical action effects and transforms our spiritual condition. As a result, sacraments are extremely powerful weapons in the ongoing battle against evil.

There are many physical actions and objects that can carry spiritual meaning and affect our spiritual condition. Candles and icons, holy buildings and sacred sites, beautiful music, architecture, and paintings can all have a wonderful spiritual effect and strengthen us spiritually. The beauties of nature, the love of our families, and the simple physical joys of life can all help us spiritually and strengthen us in the battle. But there are seven particular things that Christians recognize as having a formal sacramental effect in our life.

• *Cleansed and reborn*. On the day of Pentecost, Jesus' followers received the gift of the Holy Spirit. Peter was their appointed leader, and when he stood up to speak he explained to the crowd that to follow Christ, they needed to turn away from their selfish ways, believe in Christ, and be baptized.

Baptism is the first sacrament of the Christian life. When a person is baptized there is a spiritual dimension, faith, and a physical dimension, water. Being plunged into water symbolizes cleansing as well as rebirth. In addition, it represents the fact that by believing in Christ we are plunged into his death and resurrection.

If we are baptized as an adult, we make our own declaration of belief in Christ. This is called a "profession of faith." When a baby is baptized the profession of faith is made on his behalf by his parents and sponsors (godparents).

As the person is plunged into the water or has water poured over him, the person performing the Baptism proclaims that this solemn action is done in the name of the Father, the Son, and the Holy Spirit. This is to show that through Baptism we enter into the very life of God himself, and God's life enters into us.

The sacrament of Baptism cleanses us from that inborn tendency to do wrong called Original Sin. It also gives us the power to live God's way and decide to follow his will in our lives. At that point the Holy Spirit begins to work in our lives to enable us to take part in the great battle against evil, sin, and death.

• *Sealed in faith*. In the sacrament of *Confirmation*, a baptized person is formally received into the Church. After a suitable time of instruction the baptized person decides that he wants to be a full member of the Church. At that point a bishop or priest lays his hands on the person's head and anoints him with blessed oil. This formal blessing symbolizes the Father's blessing of his child, and through this physical/spiritual action a person is made a full member of the Church family.

In a way, what was begun at Baptism is completed at Confirmation. At that point the person makes sure, or confirms, his earlier decision, or the decision that was made for him by his parents if he was baptized as an infant.

• *Forgiven and freed*. At Baptism God cleanses us from Original Sin and gives us the power to fight the good fight of faith. But in that war we often lose battles. It is not easy to follow Christ, and we fight against powerful enemies. The spiritual forces of darkness will do their best to make us fall into selfishness and sin.

We also have to fight against our own fallen nature. Baptism gives us the power to fight, but it doesn't mean we are made perfect overnight. Our own effort, our cooperation with the power of the Holy Spirit, is required if we are to win the battle.

When we fail, members of our team pick us up and help us keep going. Remember, we are fighting as part of a great army, and it is part of an army's duty to set up ambulances, rescue teams, and field hospitals to help those who have fallen in battle. When we fall back into the darkness of selfishness, lust, anger, and violence, we have a way back into a good relationship with God. *Forgiveness* is God's way of putting us back into the same clean and whole condition we first received at our Baptism.

We receive that forgiveness through the sacrament of *Reconciliation*, or *Confession*. Confession is a powerful weapon in the battle against evil. Jesus gave his disciples the power to forgive sins on earth just as he had done, and that power continues to be present and available to us through the ministry of the priest in the sacrament of Reconciliation. After we confess our sins to God, the priest, by the power Christ gave the Church, solemnly pronounces God's forgiveness. Through that gift we get a fresh start, the power to change and continue our fight against evil.

• *Healing, inside and out.* When Jesus was on earth his power to forgive was always linked with his power to heal. Since the Church is the body of Christ on earth, the Church still has the power to do what Christ did. The Church is our army in the battle. It is there to help us be equipped, to fight well, and to be healed when we've been wounded.

Of course, in a general way we can be healed through medical technology and the work of professional physicians, but along with this obvious form of healing are some wonderful aspects of healing within the ministry of the Church. Some people in the Church have a counseling ministry. These people help us to find inner healing. Others have the ministry of spiritual direction. They help us to find spiritual healing and strength. Still others have the gift of physical healing.

There is also a formal sacrament of healing: the *Anointing of the Sick*. In this sacrament the physical element is blessed oil. The spiritual element is turning from our own way and having faith in

Christ's healing power. The formal sacrament of healing is usually reserved for cases of extreme illness, and many priests and people report that real, physical healings often take place when the sacrament is administered.

In other cases people are healed in an inner way. They may find new relief from pain, greater peace of mind, and a new strength to cope with their illness. Often the family members of those who are anointed also find new strength and spiritual help in their time of need.

When a person is anointed at the very end of his life it is sometimes called *Extreme Unction*, or the *last rites*. Sometimes the sacrament actually brings the person back from death's door for a longer period of life. More often the last rites prepare the person for a peaceful death and assure him that his sins are forgiven, that all shall be well, and that he can depart in peace.

• *Forming a new squadron.* In every army there are subgroups — small, united, well-bonded fighting units. This is not a bad way to think of a Christian family. God loves to work through the power of human love and family ties. When a man, a woman, and children are bound together in the deep and abiding love of *marriage* they make up a powerful fighting force.

The powers of evil hate pure, solid, and sensible family love. That is why they tempt us with sexual sin: because they do not want us to be part of a happy marriage. They do not want children born into the world if they are going to be born into a solid, faithful Christian family.

Christians have always been devoted to building up the family. The sexual instincts are a powerful force. Through them love is expressed and comes to abundance in the lives of new children. Within Christian marriage and family life there is great fruitfulness, great power for good, and therefore a great potential for victory over evil. Forming a Christian marriage is therefore one of the best ways anyone can fight against the powers of evil in the world.

That is why the Church has said that Marriage is a sacrament. In Marriage the physical and the spiritual are joined in a marvelous and miraculous way. When a husband and wife make love they are sealing with a physical action a union that is spiritual and eternal. When they conceive, bear, and raise children, they are fostering new human beings with immortal souls, made in God's image.

• *Taking orders.* In the Christian battle there are some people who are professional soldiers. These are the ones who are uniquely dedicated to the battle. They have no other claims on their time. They are the specialists and the experts. They are available to go anywhere and serve God totally in the battle against evil.

When a man is ordained as a priest, or when a man or a woman becomes a monk or a nun, they are specially dedicated to serving God only. This is why, in most cases, they also take a vow of celibacy. This vow doesn't mean they think sex is wrong. They believe sex is wonderful, but that it belongs to marriage and family life. Because they have decided to serve God alone, they have given up family life and therefore have given up sexual relationships.

The formal sacrament of Ordination, or *Holy Orders*, is reserved for those men who judge themselves called by God to be priests. The priesthood is reserved to men not because women are inferior, but because Jesus, who founded the priesthood, chose men only to be priests. In the Church sometimes different roles are appropriate only for men or for women. This is not considered discrimination but rather a reflection of God's design.

Likewise, priests are not superior to lay people or vice versa, but we all fulfill our special roles as equal members of God's family. In a sense all Christians are called to be "priests" because all of us are called to fight the good fight of faith and minister God's love to the world. But we are not all *ordained* as priests because, within the battle, we exercise our priesthood in a multitude of ways.

When a priest is ordained, the bishop and other priests lay hands on his head and he is anointed with oil for his new role in life. This is the physical aspect of the sacrament. The spiritual element is the man's calling, dedication to service, and faithful vow to serve Christ.

In each of these sacraments, we are given a physical/spiritual weapon to help us in our physical/spiritual lives. The seven sacraments are God's way of helping us through every stage and decision point in our lives. From Baptism as an infant through Confirmation, Marriage, Reconciliation, and last rites, the Church, like an army or like a faithful family, is there to help us in the journey and equip us for the battle at hand.

But you may have noticed that I spoke of seven sacraments and discussed only six. The seventh is the greatest and needs a separate section of its own.

THE ULTIMATE WEAPON

The Last Supper

There is one physical/spiritual weapon that is the greatest of all. The night before he died, Jesus gathered his Apostles together and celebrated a special ceremonial meal with them.

As we discussed earlier, when the Jewish people were enslaved in Egypt God told them to sacrifice a young lamb and put its blood on the doorposts and lintels of their houses. When the angel of death saw the blood he would pass over their homes and spare them. Forever after that, the Jewish people celebrated the same "Passover" meal every year. They killed a lamb, which they called the Lamb of God, and as they ate the ceremonial meal, they relived their salvation from death and their delivery from slavery.

Jesus' last meal with his Apostles was this Passover meal. At the meal they read the Old Testament story of the Passover, then celebrated the meal once again. At the meal they ate the lamb that had been sacrificed and also ate bread and drank wine. As they shared this ancient ceremonial meal Jesus added a new dimension to it.

Jesus took the bread, blessed it, and broke it. He then said, "This is my Body, which is given up for you. Do this in remembrance of me." Then he took the cup, blessed the wine, and said, "This is my Blood of the new covenant. Drink this in remembrance of me."[46]

Remember, the word *covenant* means a sacred promise or a solemn agreement between two parties. John the Baptist had called Jesus the Lamb of God, and there at the Passover supper Jesus said he was going to die for his friends. *He* was therefore the Lamb of God who would be killed to deliver them from death and slavery. The old covenant was centered on the ritual sacrifice of animals in the Temple. Jesus inaugurated the New Covenant by sacrificing himself — one time for all humanity — on the Cross.

Jesus transformed the Jewish ceremonial meal into a new kind of meal. The new ritual would be not to commemorate the ancient delivery from slavery and death, but to commemorate the delivery from slavery and death that he was to accomplish. Likewise he transformed the Temple sacrifice into a new kind of sacrifice, carried out on the altar at Mass and in the temple of our bodies. Jesus

---

[46] Cf. Luke 22:19, 20.

told his Apostles to celebrate this physical/spiritual covenant, or sacrament, until the end of time.

I Am with You

Jesus also promised his Apostles that he would be with them until the end of time. After he rose from the dead his Apostles realized that he was with them in an astounding way through the ceremonial meal that he had commanded them to continue.

In a disturbing lesson, Jesus had told his followers that they could not have life within them unless they ate his Flesh and drank his Blood. Obviously he was not telling them to be cannibals, so what could he possibly have meant? It all became clear when he celebrated the Passover meal with them. When he said the bread was his Flesh and the wine was his Blood they remembered that he had said they couldn't have spiritual life within them unless they ate his Flesh and drank his Blood.

This same ceremonial meal-sacrifice has been continued for the last two thousand years. In a multitude of ways all over the earth every day this sacred meal is celebrated with reverence, devotion, and care. Why do Christians take such care and spend so much time on this strange ceremony involving bread and wine?

It is because we really believe that Jesus Christ, who lived and died and rose again, is with us through the bread and wine. In fact, we believe that the bread and wine have been transformed into his Body and Blood. We do not believe that if you took the bread and wine into a laboratory it would turn out to be human flesh and blood. Instead, we believe that its inner reality is transformed by God's power into Jesus' Flesh and Blood, his soul and divinity. One way to explain what we believe happens is to say that the bread's "bread-ness" and the wine's "wine-ness" has become the Flesh and Blood of Jesus Christ.

Christianity Pure and Simple

The sacraments are all physical/spiritual realities. They are not just symbols. They are not just good ideas. We have bodies and souls blended together. Both are real. Therefore, God chooses to work in us through real bread and real wine that have really been transformed by Christ's action into his own Body and Blood.

Battle Rations

Every army needs battle rations. Every pilgrim needs food for the journey. In *The Lord of the Rings* the travelers are given a special bread called *lembas* that never gets stale and gives them supernatural endurance. In the Old Testament exodus story the Jewish people were given *manna* — a special bread from heaven for their journey through the wilderness. When he was on earth Jesus fed a crowd by miraculously multiplying bread and fish.

When Jesus told his Apostles to celebrate the memorial meal — the sacrificial ritual — until the end of time, he was commanding them to provide supernatural food for the troops. The successors of the Apostles are the bishops and the priests of the Church. By a direct historical line every Catholic priest can trace the fact that by his ordination he is descended from the Apostles. Because of this, he is the one who is authorized to preside at the celebration of this ceremonial meal that is called the Eucharist, or the Mass.

The bread and wine do not become Christ's Body and Blood by the priest alone. Instead the risen and present Lord Jesus Christ performs the miracle through the priest. When he does so, we receive our physical/spiritual food for the journey. When we eat the bread and wine that have been transformed into Christ's Body and Blood, we receive Christ in a unique and powerful way. The elements enter our body and our bloodstream, and we receive physical and spiritual strength from them.

Christ is with us in this way more powerfully and wonderfully than we ever could have imagined. This is not simply a religious symbol or a spiritual idea. It is a *reality*. Many Christians will relate how the spiritual strength conferred by the Eucharist has helped them make their way through life.

The Power to Change

It has been said, "You will become like the thing you worship." This assumes that all of us worship something; but often we are not aware of what we worship. The way to figure out what we worship is to ask ourselves what it is that we live for and what it is that we would be willing to die for. That is the thing we worship.

Do we worship our job? We might think that we are not willing to die for our boss, but if we devote so much time and energy to our job that it is slowly killing us, then maybe we are willing to die for our job. Do we worship the money that our job brings? Do we worship pleasure? If we are willing to risk our lives for that pleasure (through smoking, overindulgence, promiscuous sex, or drugs), then we are willing to die for that thing.

Jesus Christ simply asks us to get our priorities right and to worship the only One who is worthy of our worship: God. *Eucharist* means "thanksgiving," and when we go to the Eucharist we are worshiping God and giving thanks for all he has done in our lives.

We do this by worshiping Jesus Christ, who is God in human form. If we become like the thing we worship, then we choose to worship Jesus Christ because, as the God-Man, he is the one we want to be like. As we receive him into our lives by eating his Body and drinking his Blood in the Eucharist, we really do receive the power to become like him.

This is what worship is all about, and by focusing on Christ in the Eucharist, we immediately put other false objects of worship into their rightful place. That's why we are expected to go to Mass every week: because we need a constant correction of our priorities. To fight well, we need to get focused and get our bearings time and time again.

Getting Focused

When we go attend Mass every week we focus on the reason we're on this earth. We don't go for sensual pleasure. We don't go for financial profit. We don't go to fulfill some arbitrary religious requirement, and try not to be bored. We go for a purpose. We go to join in the fight against the powers of darkness and evil.

We cannot do this unless we bind ourselves to Christ, who already won the victory against evil. We do this first in Baptism and Confirmation, but we renew our covenant with Christ through the sacrament of Reconciliation, and by receiving Communion regularly.

During Mass we hear several passages of the Bible as they are read. The priest speaks for a short time to give us advice in the physical/spiritual battle we are a part of. The Bible is God's word to us. When we hear the Bible at Mass we are receiving spiritual food for our mind and soul.

After that, the priest performs a ritual recalling the Last Supper and Christ's Sacrifice on the Cross, and then we all celebrate the holy meal together. Just as Christ did, the priest takes the bread, breaks it, and blesses it. He then gives it to us as food for the journey and as the living presence of Christ in our lives.

This sacrament ought to be central to the lives of all Christians, since Christianity is first and foremost about staying in touch with Christ, and keeping his Spirit alive in us. Receiving him in this physical/spiritual way at Mass is the most vibrant, real, and powerful way to stay in touch with him.

Taking Action

Now, the sacraments are our weapons in the battle; they are not the end or goal of the fight. They are given to help us live a new kind of life, not to *be* that life.

The sacraments equip and strengthen us for the battle, but we actually engage in the Christian battle by living our lives day by day. Within our daily lives there are many ways to fight the battle, and I would now like to turn from the weapons to the battle itself.

CHANGING YOURSELF

Good In Means Good Out

Your spiritual life is like a mill. You put grain in, and you get flour out. If you don't put something good in, you can't get something good out. It's as simple as that. Our minds need to be filled with good things if our lives are going to yield a good product.

In our media-saturated world it is difficult not to have our minds filled with lots of images and sounds. Of course, much of the content of popular music, television, films, and magazines is simply harmless fun. It entertains and amuses us, and that's good. But some of it is garbage, worthless trivia that occupies space on our mind's hard drive that should be used for something better; or worse, genuine trash that poisons our imagination and pollutes our minds with violent, pornographic, or materialistic images and desires.

If we are fighting a spiritual battle, we will make sure that we fill our minds instead with things that are good, true, and beautiful. We should take time for the natural goodness of the world around us. We should open our minds to the best music, literature, and art. We should learn to enjoy all that builds us up and opens our minds to the best in other cultures. One of the best ways to win this aspect of the battle is to take time to read good books that engage our minds with ideas in a fresh way.

For a Christian, one of the key sources of learning and enlightenment is the documents of the faith. The writings of the saints, the words of worship, and the Bible all contribute to building up the mind and putting in goodness so goodness can come out.

The Good Book

The Bible contains two main sections: the Old Testament and the New Testament. The Old Testament records the religious history of the Jewish people, as well as their religious poetry, sayings, sermons, and hymns. The New Testament begins with four versions of the story of Jesus Christ, called the Gospels. The rest of the New Testament is the story of the foundation of the Christian Church and letters of instruction that the apostles wrote to the first Christians.

Christians believe that the Bible is *inspired* by God. This does not mean we believe it was dropped out of heaven. Nor was it dictated to the human writers by an angel or the Holy Spirit. Instead, the Spirit inspired, or "breathed into," the writers in a more subtle way. The Holy Spirit infused the biblical authors with the insights and ideas he wanted to communicate and the power to express them properly. We also believe that the same Holy Spirit uses the Bible today to inspire and enlighten us as we read it.

Pick Up and Read

Therefore every Christian should have a Bible and read it. It is difficult, however, to decide how and when to read the Bible. Some people simply start at the beginning and read a chapter a day. But the most difficult parts of the Bible are at the beginning, and many people get bogged down after only a week or two.

The Great Battle

The best way to read the Bible is to read it with the whole Church, day by day and week by week. When we go to Mass each Sunday, a section of the Old Testament, an ancient Jewish hymn called a psalm, and a section of the New Testament are read. Then a portion from one of the Gospels is read. All these weekly portions are collected in a book called a missal. If you have a missal you will have handy and accessible portions of the Bible to read day by day and week by week.

Other people use Bible reading guides, often published in little magazines that you can buy in Christian bookstores or order by mail. These give you a portion of the Bible to read every day and provide a few paragraphs to explain the Bible passage and apply it to your life.

It is possible to study the Bible in great depth, or simply to read it to learn more about your faith. But either way, the Bible is best read in an atmosphere of prayer. You should ask the Holy Spirit to open your eyes to the truths in the Bible and to help you understand what you read and apply it in your life.

The wisdom and the words of the Bible really do have a power to transform lives, and if you want to get energy and light for the battle against the darkness, then read the Bible and learn how to pray.

Keeping in Touch

Prayer is vital not just when we're reading the Bible, but for the whole spiritual life. No one can grow as a Christian without learning how to pray, and we learn how to pray as we learn how to swim or how ride a bike — by regular practice.

Many people's ideas of prayer are linked with a childhood understanding of prayer. They imagine that prayer consists of asking God for things they want. Certainly there is one dimension of prayer that consists of asking God for what we want, but prayer is much greater than that. Someone has well said, "Prayer doesn't change God; it changes me."

In other words, we pray first and foremost to align ourselves with God's will. When Jesus taught his disciples to pray he instructed them to say to God, "May your will be done on earth as it is in heaven."[47] In other words, they were subjecting their own will to God's will. Through prayer they were trying to find out what God wanted — not tell him what *they* wanted. That's why, when a Christian asks God for anything, he ends the request by saying, "If it is your will."

So real Christian prayer is asking God for the things that are his will. You might then ask, "What is the point? If it is his will, won't it happen anyway?"

But there is a mysterious action going on in prayer. When we pray we align our will with God's; but we sometimes forget that the human will is a very strong power in the world. When we align our will with God's the two together become a powerful force for good. If you look at it this way, prayer is like surfing. God's will is the big wave coming in. I am trying to find out where it's going, then to go with it and ride the wave.

Purifying the Mind

Many religions teach their followers to meditate. Meditation is known to have marvelous beneficial effects. People who meditate regularly have less stress. They live longer. They are happier, and they deal with problems in a more confident way. People who meditate enjoy better health, better relationships, and a better quality of life.

[47]Cf. Matthew 6:10.

In the Eastern religions the meditation technique is to empty the mind and simply dwell in the eternal silence. This activity slows down the mind waves and allows the person who is meditating to enter into a calmer, more peaceful state of being.

Christians use the word *meditation* for another kind of mental activity. When Christians meditate they take a story from the Gospels or a word or phrase from the Bible, and they "bathe" themselves in that idea, phrase, or mental image. They relax into the particular phrase or idea or image until it goes deep into them and they become part of it.

Many Christians use the Rosary as a way of doing this. The Rosary is a pattern of prayers, usually kept track of with a string of beads. These prayers help to calm the mind and take the person to a deeper state of consciousness. At the same time, the person focuses on a particular event in the lives of Jesus and Mary, his mother. As we say the prayers and enter into this deeper state we also enter more deeply into the life, ministry, death, and resurrection of Jesus. In this way our life is merged with his life and we become more like him.

This is a more positive and objective form of meditation than the Eastern religions practice. It doesn't call for an empty mind and a focus on nothingness, but for a mind full and focused on real and powerful content. Christian meditation is just as calming and peaceful as Eastern meditation, but it is also meaningful, and as such, it is a simple and effective way to get closer to Christ and engage in the spiritual battle against evil.

The Still Point of the Turning World

The Christian practice that is more like the meditation of Eastern religions is what we call *contemplation*. In contemplative prayer a person is taken beyond meditation on a particular image,

phrase, or story. When a person enters into contemplation he simply dwells in the presence of Christ.

This sounds rather strange. It isn't. Have you ever spent an
evening with someone you love and realize that you don't have to
talk or play a game or go out somewhere? It is fine simply to together. Maybe you are reading together or doing a puzzle or knit-
ting. You don't need to talk to one another. You can simply be
together.

Contemplation is like that, except that the other person we are
with is Jesus Christ. In the forms of meditation taught by the Eastern religions the person meditating is supposed to empty his mind,
but in Christian contemplation we fill our mind with the presence
of Christ.

An old peasant woman was asked how she prays. She said, "I
just sit and look at him, and he sits and looks at me." That simple
peasant was a real contemplative, and her words fit in with the
experience of millions of Christians. One of the greatest saints of
modern times, a young French woman named Thérèse Martin,
said that contemplation was to "gaze on the face of Christ."

Another way to gaze on the face of Christ is in the traditional
service of Benediction, or adoration of the Blessed Sacrament. In
this simple act of worship the consecrated bread from the Eucharist is displayed on the altar in a large receptacle called a *mon-
strance*. The simple white disk, which is truly the Body of Christ,
becomes the focus point for our contemplation, and through this
action we enter into his presence in a way far beyond all words and
description.

Communities of Prayer

Prayer is so important to the spiritual struggle that there are
communities of people who live together to devote their lives

entirely to prayer. Monks and nuns give up all other ambitions in order to spend their whole lives in prayer.

This doesn't mean they spend every moment of every day on their knees in church. Instead they try to live a life in which prayer is the heartbeat of every moment. Monks and nuns *do* spend much time in actual prayer, but they are also trying to bring prayer into every moment of life so that every action and thought also becomes totally given to God, and so becomes a kind of prayer.

There are a vast number of different communities of prayer all over the world. Some are for men only, some for women only. Some have married couples and families living together with celibate people. Some are totally enclosed and traditional. In these communities the men and women rarely go out; they pursue a totally inner life of study and prayer.

Other communities are more modern and are engaged in activities to promote the Christian faith, to work for justice and peace, and to help the disadvantaged, the disabled, and the poor. In these communities the devoted men and women combine prayer with action in a life of total dedication.

These special communities are part of the whole Church, but each local church or parish is also supposed to be a community of prayer. As we meet together with one another and in our own homes, we are constantly fighting the battle against evil by learning how to pray.

Getting Together

The local community gets together every week to do together what each Christian should have been doing on his own throughout the week. At Mass we pray, read the Bible, focus on Christ, and recommit ourselves to the battle we first signed up for in our Baptism.

Christian worship has a basic structure called the *Liturgy*. This structure, provided by the Church, is the same basic one that has been used for the last two thousand years.

In this structure we do not use our own words to worship God, but the words that are shared by the whole of God's family. Using a set structure like this does two things. First, it ensures that the words of worship are purely Christian, and that they have not been infected with false ideas. Second, it binds us together with all other Christians who have used and are using these same words.

While we use the same set structure, the actual worship might vary somewhat. The music and style of using these words can be very different depending on where you go. Therefore, in one place the Mass may be a solemn High Mass with classical music and a fine choir. In another place the music will be provided by a group of local people playing instruments and singing simple hymns. If you go to Africa or South America the style will be very different still, but the basic structure and the content will be the same.

This unity in the midst of diversity is one of the great strengths of the Catholic Church. In it we can all worship the same Lord Jesus Christ. We can all commit to the same battle, and yet we can also be ourselves and worship God in a language and style that is right for us.

CHANGING THE WORLD

What's the Point?

Prayer, worship, and reading are not the end goal of the practice of the Christian religion. Like the sacraments, they are only the means to an end. We do these things because they bring us into a closer relationship with God, by whom our lives are transformed. By prayer, worship, and the practice of religious sacraments, God works in our lives, and we gradually grow into the people we were created to be.

Yet Christianity has never simply been about personal ful-fillment or salvation. From the very beginning, Christianity, like the Jewish faith from which it developed, has been a *communal* religion.

It is impossible to be a totally solitary Christian. To be a Chris-tian means we belong to the Body of Christ and that Body is made up of all the other people in the world and down the ages who have also followed Christ. To be a Christian means belonging to the Christian family, made up of those alive in the world today and those who have gone before us.

So, being a Christian means we are involved with all other people. We are called to be concerned about their welfare and to do as much as we can to help them. We do not ask God to change us through prayer, worship, and personal renewal just for our own gratification. We ask him to change us so that we can also go on to change the world.

Missionaries of Charity

Mother Teresa of Calcutta was an excellent example of how prayer and action can go together. Mother Teresa was a nun. Her life was devoted to prayer, meditation, and contemplation. For many years she taught in a convent school for middle-class Indian girls. If Mother Teresa had been interested only in her own salva-tion she would not have had the eyes to see the suffering of others. But through her prayer she also became aware that she should be serving the poorest of the poor in the slums of Calcutta.

Eventually she founded a little community of women who were devoted both to prayer and to a ministry to the poorest of the poor. Mother Teresa and her nuns would start each day with an hour of meditation and then worship God in the Eucharist. Each working day was punctuated with times of prayer, spiritual reading, and contemplation.

But in the middle of this life of prayer Mother Teresa and her nuns were working to change the world. They were working tirelessly to comfort the poor and dying. Mother Teresa said she *did* this because she saw the face of Christ in every poor person. She could recognize the face of Christ in the poor only because she had spent so long gazing on the face of Christ in contemplation. Mother Teresa and her nuns set an example for all Christians: prayer is the engine for changing the world.

Haves and Have Nots

Mother Teresa's work is just one example of Christianity in action. There are thousands of examples of different ways that Christians work out their own salvation by ministering to others. Down through history more schools, hospitals, clinics, universities, and food banks have been started and staffed by Christians than by all other groups put together. Driven by their life of prayer, and motivated by the example of Jesus Christ, Christians have been at the forefront of the battle against poverty, disease, and injustice in all its forms.

Those who work with the poor are the front-line soldiers. There are others who work from home, administering charities, educating the public about the needs of the poor, and working hard not just to treat the symptoms, but to address the root problems of poverty.

This Christian battle against poverty goes on in every country, in cities and in the countryside. It goes on where famine and disaster strike and where ordinary conditions force people to live lives of misery and squalor.

The Great Battle

If you want to change the world, there are many ways your Christian faith can help you get involved and make a difference.

Peace and Justice

Besides working to relieve poverty, Christians are also busy trying to establish peace and justice in the world, through social and political activism. This, too, is Christianity in action. Furthermore, the Christian who prays and worships is committed to working for peace and justice *in his own life*. He should constantly ask himself if he is doing enough to live a simple life, to help the poor, and to exhibit love and kindness toward his family, friends, and neighbors.

Imagine what the world would be like if everyone were honest. Imagine what the world would be like if everyone did their best, never made a quarrel worse, and always sought for fairness and justice for all. What a wonderful world it would be!

We cannot make such a world overnight, but if every Christian person were to take his faith seriously and try even a little bit harder, the world would be a better place for everyone.

Reconciliation and Forgiveness

I cannot change the world, but with God's help I can change myself. I cannot take away all the suffering and pain in the world, but I can start by eliminating the pain and suffering that I cause other people.

If Christians take their faith seriously, they must always be on the lookout for ways to make things better within their own lives and within their own relationships. Our hearts are constantly tempted by jealousy, pride, envy, hatred, bitterness, and the desire for revenge. It is the responsibility of Christians to address these problems in their own hearts, in their own lives, and in their own relationships.

If we were to allow the Holy Spirit to rule our lives and direct us, we would have the strength to reach out in forgiveness to those who have offended us. We would have the courage to build new relationships of love and justice. We would have the insight to be happy with what we have rather than seeking for more, more, more.

The Christian faith is practical. It works. All the religious activity is meant to get us to the point at which Jesus Christ will be so much a part of us that he will work through us to bring about his will in the world. The battle against evil really can be won. Suffering really can be defeated. The world can be changed. And the change starts right where I am at this present moment.

Starting Where We Are

Mother Teresa started where *she* was. She was just another nun teaching in a school for girls. Once she got permission to start working among the poor she moved to a slum in Calcutta and did what she could do. She was a teacher. She started teaching the slum children. She didn't have any training as a nurse, so she got some and started ministering to the health needs of the poor as well. Eventually some of her former students came to help her, and the now-famous order of nuns came into being.

Each one of us can begin to change ourselves and to change the world, and we can start where we are. Every journey begins with the first step. It might seem that you are a nobody. Wonderful. It is always people who know they are nobody who change the world for the best. It might seem that you have no gifts. The best gifts are not wealth, education, and brilliance, but a heart and mind totally transformed by the power of the Holy Spirit.

Right now, this very day, you can decide to change yourself and follow Christ into the amazing future he has prepared for you.

Right now, this very day, you can decide to work with him to change the world as much as you can. Right where you are, you can decide to make the most of your gifts and the most of who you are and spend the rest of your life making the world a better place. Whoever you are, you can decide to fight the great fight against evil, or give in to that evil.

Climb Every Mountain

No one promises that the fight will be easy. Indeed, deciding to fight against evil and live for Christ might be the hardest thing you will ever decide to do. You will constantly stumble and fall in your effort to live a better life. That's okay. It doesn't matter how often you fall. It matters how often you get up.

If you decide to live the Christian life, you will discover that the Church is full of hypocrites. Other Christians will let you down. Some Christian leaders will turn out to be sinners and shallow, self-centered frauds. Some of your Christian friends will show themselves to be weak-willed, lazy, and unwilling to help in the battle. Then, if you have any insight, you will realize that they are all just like you.

Don't imagine that the Christian life will be a nice, easy life full of wonderful spiritual experiences and "happy religious time." You will get discouraged. There will be dark times. Remember, you are engaged in a war. You may think at times that you will never win. You may despair as you lose battle after battle. You may be tempted to give up, and at the end you will be convinced that the darkness is greater than the light.

In fact, like climbing a mountain, the further you go on this journey, the harder it will become. But also like climbing a mountain, the further you go, the better the views get. The air is clearer, and you become stronger and more resolute.

Are you up to the challenge? As I've said, no one can do it alone. That is why we are accompanied and helped on the journey by all the others who have also decided to follow Christ. The final section of this book will help you explore the Church in more detail, and help you to understand more about the amazing army of God that becomes your new family.

Chapter Five

Welcome Home

FAMILY OF GOD

One of the most famous stories Jesus Christ told was about a runaway son. The boy went to his wealthy father and asked for his inheritance money early. The doting father gave him some cash, and the boy ran off and wasted it on parties and pleasure.

When the money ran out the boy's friends ran out, too. Hard times hit the city, and soon the boy was stuck with no money, no friends, no qualifications, and no future. He ended up taking a job as a pig farmer and had to fight the pigs to get enough food to eat. Then he remembered his father.

At that point Jesus says the boy "came to himself."[48] He saw himself and his circumstances as they really were. He realized how good he'd had it at home. Even his father's servants were better off than he was then. If he were to go home and volunteer to be a servant in his father's house, perhaps he would at least have a decent meal every day.

The boy started on the long road home. As he approached he saw that his father was at the front gate waiting and watching for his return. The father rejoiced at his son's return, forgave him everything, and welcomed him home with a great feast.

[48]Luke 15:7.

Christianity Pure and Simple

When a person decides to change his life and follow God's way instead of his own selfish way, it is just like the homecoming of that runaway son. Every time we take a step toward God and away from our own selfishness, it is as if we have arrived home. Part of us is complete. A deep dark corner of our lives is touched with light, and we begin to glimpse the possibility of finding the peace we have always looked for.

Brothers and Sisters Abounding

The apostle Paul said that to come home like this was to become a member of the family of God. He recognized that all human beings are the fugitive sons and daughters of God, and that to be restored to the family we first have to turn toward home.

This is a *reality*, not just a theory or a nice way of talking. Once we turn from our way and accept Christ's way, once we believe that Christ died to give us new life, a real transformation takes place in our relationship with God. Like runaways we have come home, and the Father welcomes us with open arms. As the father did in the story, God then gives us an array of good gifts.

This new relationship with God means we also enter into a new relationship with every other person down through the centuries who has ever followed Jesus Christ. For two thousand years people have made the same decision. They have also heard God's call and decided to leave everything and follow him. They, too, returned home and were welcomed into the family of God.

We therefore have a bond with all Christians down through the ages. They are not alive on this earth, but they are alive on the other side, and they are interested in us and the rest of God's family. These people who have been totally transformed by Christ's loving power are the saints. In Christ they are our older brothers and sisters.

Making New Old Friends

The saints make up a vast and varied collection of people. There are saints from every walk of life, from every class, race, and nationality. Children, old people, soldiers, nuns, politicians, and priests have all become saints. Parents, husbands and wives, scholars and simpletons, princes and peasants have all become saints. The vast array of saints shows us that anyone who is willing can be totally transformed by Christ.

The Bible calls the saints a "great cloud of witnesses."[49] The word used for "witness" is the same word for "martyr"; and in their own way all the saints have learned to give up their lives for Christ. Some of them literally gave up their lives at the hands of violent men. Others gave up their lives more quietly, in the service of others and in constant self-giving.

The saints still work with Christ for the redemption of the world, even though they are in heaven, not on earth. As we fight the battle against evil we become aware that we do not fight alone. Our older brothers and sisters in the faith love us and fight with us in the great battle.

As we begin walking in the Christian life it will not be long before we learn more about certain saints. Their lives will appeal to us. We will want to learn more about how they followed Christ and will desire to follow their example. As we do, we will feel that the saints are with us as friends and fellow travelers in the journey.

Unity and Diversity

We can't see the saints, but we know that they are with us because they are alive in God, and God is always with us. They are present during our prayers. They are present at the Mass, where we

[49]Hebrews 12:1.

recognize their presence and pray with them. They are present with us as we contemplate their lives and deeds. We soon become aware that we do not worship alone, but we worship with a great cloud of witnesses surrounding us.

I mention the saints in heaven first because it is vital to remember that being a Christian joins us with people who have been alive and active in the world for the last two thousand years. What we do here and now is connected with what has gone before.

Once we are aware of our relationship with all the saints of the past we will better understand our relationship with all the other Christians in the present. When we become Catholic we do not simply join our local church. The Catholic Church is vast, and just as there has been a huge variety of saints through the ages, today there is a broad range of people within it all around the world.

Within the vast range of national groups, races, classes, and abilities there is yet a remarkable unity. Down through the ages, political rulers have tried to establish worldwide power — an empire, political network, or universal brotherhood that included all people. In the Catholic Church it already exists. Within the Church all people can exist together as brothers and sisters in Christ.

Groups and Subgroups

Because of the vast range of people in a local parish it's sometimes difficult to feel at home. A Catholic church sometimes feels more like a bus stop than a family gathering — a wide variety of people gathered for the same practical reason, who otherwise don't seem to belong together at all.

It is vital to take an active part in our local parish because that is where we learn to get along with other Catholics who might be very different from us. But it is also important to realize that within the Catholic Church there are many smaller groups and subgroups. Think of the Catholic Church as a huge tree, with many different branches and twigs. Along with active parish involvement, many Catholics also find a group or subgroup within the Church where they find others with shared interests and outlooks.

There are groups for young people and groups for the elderly. Some nurture prayer, spirituality, Christian growth, and evangelization. Others focus on church worship and music. Some help build marriages and family life. Others are involved in education, health care, ecology, and concern for the poor. Still others look after children, foster adoption, and work to eliminate the crime of abortion. All these groups are Catholic. Some of them are well established. Others are exciting new movements in the Church. All of them focus on Jesus Christ in the Catholic Church, but they also have their own priorities, aims, and ways of working.

Parish life is where the ordinary, day-to-day spiritual life takes place, and it mustn't be neglected, but seeking out one of the groups within the Catholic Church will help you feel at home. It will provide a way for your spiritual life to go forward by leaps and bounds. The others in that group will help you feel part of the larger family, and as you get involved with them in the life of Christ you will realize that this kind of unity and commitment is what makes life worthwhile.

Fitting In, Not Sticking Out

It will not always be easy to stay with the Catholic Church. Sometimes other churches may seem more attractive and happier places to be. But joining the Catholic Church is a serious business. It is like marriage. You make the promises for better or for worse. It is no good flitting from one church to another, any more than it is a good idea to flit from one marriage to another.

Throughout our relationship with the Church the difficulties are actually part of the larger test. This process helps us to grow spiritually. To be a Catholic means to accept that the Church is bigger, older, and wiser than we are. It means we don't set out to change the Church, but we allow the Church to change us. We realize that the Church is the creation of Jesus and belongs to him.

A person does not join the Catholic Church because it is the church with the best music or the nicest people or the most interesting sermons. If you want nice music, go to a concert. If you want nice people, join a country club. If you want good speeches, join a speakers' club. But if you want to belong to the fullest expression of the Body of Christ on earth, become a Catholic.

Finding our place in the Church is necessary because the whole point of the Christian life is to go with God. By fitting into our place in the Church, we put our own will to the side. We try to be humble and say, "Maybe I don't always know best. I'm going to try to learn from the difficulty. I'm going to find God right here — not somewhere else." Then we start to learn that the best way to discover God is by finding our rightful place within the vast and beautiful unity that is the one, holy, catholic, and apostolic Church.

THE ONE CHURCH

Longing for Unity

When we perceive chaos and disorder in the world, it makes us frustrated and angry. It is part of human nature to want things to fit together. We want to find meaning in the universe. We want all that is broken to be mended, all that is wounded to be healed, and all that is divided to be reconciled. In other words, we want *unity*.

Even within ourselves we long for unity. Our worldly ambitions clash with our spiritual goals. The desires of our body war against the better ideals of our soul. Our mental ideas and viewpoint don't fit the reality of life.

We also long for unity in our relationships. We want our families and friends to live together in peace and harmony, not in anger and bitterness. We long for unity in our communities, in our nation, and in our world. We don't want to see the destruction caused by war, violence, hatred, and selfishness.

This longing for unity reaches to the whole world. We sense that the world is divided and that various elements are at war with one another, and we wish for true peace, harmony, and unity to prevail. When we say that we believe in "one Church" we profess our belief that the unity we long for exists in the Christian Church. That unity is not perfect yet, but in the Church we can get a glimpse of the unity that all human beings should share.

One Lord, One Faith, One Baptism

In the New Testament the Christian leader Paul said, "There is one body, one Spirit, one Lord, one faith, one baptism."[50] When we are baptized we enter into that one Body. We trust that one faith and join our divided selves with this greater unity that exists within God's will. Elsewhere Paul said the Church is the Body of Christ, and that each member is a part of that body. Jesus himself said there would be "one flock and one shepherd."[51]

Jesus wanted there to be one Church on earth, to be a source of reconciliation, unity, and peace for the whole of humanity. As individuals came into unity with Christ they were also coming into unity with one another, and with God's plan for the whole world. This unity is a vital sign that Jesus' message is true. Jesus prayed

[50]Cf. Ephesians 4:4, 5.
[51]Cf. John 10:16.

that his followers would be one, as he and the Father are one. This unity had to be a *visible* unity, because Jesus said others would see that unity and believe in him.

The Church is not just a club of like-minded religious people. It is more like a living organism, with its own mind and spirit and soul. That organism is united in the one faith that was given to it by Jesus Christ. All members of the organism are united by the fact that they share that faith and have been baptized into the new life of Jesus Christ. Each member everywhere in the world, from every race, language, tribe, and tradition, is united by their shared allegiance to Jesus Christ as their Lord and God.

This unity is not just a pretty word picture. It means I'm not really alone. I'm a part of every other Christian I meet. I'm a living cell in the great, cosmic Body of Christ on earth.

The Church's First Division

All Christians are united by our shared faith in Jesus Christ and our Baptism into his death and resurrection. This is a real and permanent unity that can never be destroyed. However, if the Church is the Body of Christ, that Body is wounded by division and strife. Not only is the Body wounded; it still bleeds.

During the first thousand years of the Christian faith the Church really was united. There were some breakaway groups through the centuries; there were some little factions that disagreed and separated themselves from the mainstream, but for the most part the Christian Church was united around a group of leaders, with the Bishop of Rome, the Pope, as the recognized head.

The Church's life was closely bound up with the political life of the Roman Empire, and as the Roman Empire crumbled and was divided, the Christian Church also fell into opposing camps. Increasingly, the churches in the ancient Middle East and North

Africa went their own way. Nevertheless, unity was retained under the leadership of the Bishop of Rome.

Then, at about the turn of the first millennium the conflict between the Eastern Churches in Greece, Turkey, the Middle East, and North Africa came to a head. They broke away from the ancient leadership of Rome. The Roman leaders and the Eastern Church leaders cut each other off, and a huge division in the Church took place. For complicated reasons the division still exists. Many Christians from the East — including Russia and parts of Eastern Europe — remain partially cut off from the rest of the Catholic Church.

We look to the Eastern Christians and admire them as our brothers and sisters in Christ. Like Catholics, they have retained the ancient faith that has been handed down to us from the first followers of Jesus, called Apostles. The Eastern churches have retained wonderful traditions and have endured terrible persecution. Catholics long for a reunion to take place so that the whole Church may once again breathe with the "two lungs" of East and West.

The Reformation Divides Christians Further

Five hundred years after the Eastern and Western parts of the Church divided, another terrible separation took place. In the sixteenth century, Europe was going through a time of enormous social and technological upheaval. And in some parts of the Church there was corruption, complacency, and confusion.

In the midst of this confusion came new teachings that seemed to liberate individual Christians. Fiery preachers stirred the people up with a simplified gospel message that rejected what they considered false Church teachings (such as belief in the Eucharist) and overly complicated and ornate rituals.

At the same time new political forces were rising in Europe, often at odds with the Church and jealous of its influence and wealth. The new religious thinkers joined forces with the new political leaders, and before long they had the power and support to start their own churches. In Germany the Lutherans broke away from the ancient Church. In Switzerland the Calvinists (or Presbyterians) broke away. In England dissenting groups joined the royal power to found the Church of England. There were many other smaller groups as well. Each religious teacher seemed to find something different in the Bible, and ultimately they disagreed with one another and set out to start their own churches.

Today a directory of Christian churches in the United States lists more than twenty thousand non-Catholic denominations. Surely this could not be what Christ intended when he founded one Church to reconcile all people and bring everyone into a new kind of unity for mankind!

A Wounded Church

It cannot be overestimated how much damage this division has caused the Church of Christ. The battle against evil is much more difficult if the soldiers of goodness are divided against themselves.

Catholics believe that all Christians who have faith in Christ and are baptized are in a real and substantial unity with them. However, they also recognize that the unity of Christ's Church is deeply wounded. Furthermore, the grievances of the past cannot be glossed over. We can't just pretend the problem doesn't exist.

When we honestly face the division in this way, we are not judging the goodness of other Christians. We are facing the reality that divisions of belief and practice still exist among Christians, and problems don't go away by imagining that such differences aren't important. Instead Catholics are committed to work together with our separated brothers and sisters to solve the problems of a wounded Church through dialogue, forgiveness, and self-sacrifice.

Working Toward Unity

It is important for Catholics to work together with other Christians as much as possible in the fight against evil. It is possible for Catholics to work together with non-Catholic Christians in the areas of spreading the faith, charity work, political involvement, social concerns, and regular prayer and worship.

On the formal level the Catholic Church is involved in complicated discussions with a whole range of non-Catholic Christians. Great progress is being made in resolving differences, clearing up misunderstandings, and developing new trust and friendship.

The same is possible on the local and personal level. In this age there is simply no room for Christians of various traditions to be suspicious of one another. Fighting and quarreling among Christians is a victory for the forces of evil. All of us who follow Christ are called to unity with him and unity with one another. The fact that this unity has been broken only calls for us to work harder to love and understand one another. Only in that way can we all attain to the radiant goodness and the abundant life that Jesus Christ has to offer.

THE HOLY CHURCH

Holiness and Wholeness

All of us are divided personalities. We are confused about what we really want. Our worst desires battle with our best ambitions. Our shadow self is at war with the part of us that wants the very best. The closer a person gets to resolving this inner conflict, the more mature, whole, and fulfilled he becomes.

A mature and whole person has realized that his shadow side is a distorted part of his good side. Each negative part of us is only the dark side of a genuine strength. The mature person learns how to turn stubbornness into determination, lust into love, ambition into positive power, and greed into a desire for goodness.

This is what holiness is like. In fact, the word *holiness* is linked to the word *wholeness*. When a person is holy he is whole. He is complete, mature, fully formed — all that he possibly could be. The warring elements in his nature have been reconciled. Priorities have been established, and he has learned to live at peace with himself, with God, and with others.

The Power of Perfection

We say the Church is holy not because everyone in it is perfectly saintly all the time. Anybody can see that isn't true. Instead we proclaim that the Church is holy because God's powerful grace is present in and through the Church at all times, because Jesus founded it and bound himself to it in love forever. This grace imbues the Church with a goodness and a power that are greater than the imperfections it is trying to overcome.

God's grace ministers to us through the Church as a mother helps, nurtures, and instructs her child. The child might be weak, but the mother's love is strong. We need that powerful force of goodness in our lives if we are to become like Christ. Without it we are simply trying hard to be nicer, better people, and we won't really get that far. So as one wise writer observed, "It is impossible to have God as your Father if you do not have the Church as your mother."

Because the Church is like a mother to us we sometimes compare the Church to Jesus' mother, Mary. Mary was a perfectly whole and complete person. She was holy in a natural, wise, and loving way. As she is the image of the perfectly loving and gentle mother, so she is also the image of the Church. As Mary nurtured Jesus, the Christian community nurtures us, as our teacher, our comforter, and our friend. As a mother the Church feeds us, supports us, and gives us a spiritual home.

As we receive God's grace within the Church we take great strides toward that wholeness that is called *holiness*. Those who are perfectly whole and complete in this way have great power. God radiates through their lives in an amazingly potent way. They can do great things. They can move mountains of resistance and difficulty. They can change the world. The Church is also holy, then, because it empowers people like this.

The Problem of Imperfection

But if you know anything about the Church you will protest, "Hold on a moment! The Christians I know aren't anything like that. They're a grumpy, narrow-minded group of people who are always fighting among themselves."

We should be willing to excuse the little imperfections of ordinary Christians. After all, nobody said we would be made perfect all at once. All of us are on a gradual learning curve. We're still taking the lessons and doing the practice. We might be on the right road, but we admit that we haven't arrived yet.

Of course, little imperfections are one thing, but what about the huge crimes committed by Christians — especially by Christian leaders? What are we to think when we hear of sexually criminal priests, abusive nuns, and the corrupt, power-hungry popes from centuries ago? What can we say about the history of wars, imprisonment, torture, and executions conducted in the name of Christ?

There are two answers to the problem of imperfection among Christians. First, it is fair to remember that there is a war going on.

There are forces that will do anything to destroy Christ and his Church. These powers will use the media to twist the truth and make problems seem worse than they are. To be fair we must read both sides of any story and gather facts, not just propaganda. When we look at the facts fairly the wrongdoing is often not as bad as the propaganda would make out.

Nevertheless, there have been some monstrous crimes committed by Christians — including high-ranking Christian leaders. It would be foolish to pretend otherwise. All we can say is that such crimes are not only terrible, but they are made worse because the person has professed to follow Jesus Christ. Nonetheless, it is possible to condemn the crimes of Christians but still admit the truth of their message. When a person doesn't live up to the ideal it doesn't mean the ideal was wrong.

Don't Forget the War

But are you really surprised when good people do bad things? Good people are those who are most involved in the battle against evil, and in any war there will be some major casualties. Sometimes the enemy will win a major battle (even though he will never win the war).

While God's grace is at work, human selfishness, greed, anger, and violence are also still at work. The war between good and evil is always present, and when you think about it, where else would the war claim the most casualties but on the front line — within the army of those most committed to goodness, truth, and light?

We mustn't excuse the wrongdoing or underplay its seriousness, but did we really think that all Christians were going to be squeaky clean and victorious all the time? Wouldn't you be suspicious if the history of the Church were claimed to be 100 percent perfect? If it were, it couldn't be real.

Seeing What Can Be

Furthermore, whenever we pick out the bad things Christians have done we have to be fair and also see the good things, too. For every immoral cleric today there are a hundred chaste nuns who give their lives to serve the poor. For every corrupt pope in history there have been thousands of holy, hard-working, self-sacrificing popes, bishops, and priests.

The Church's holiness is real, even though it is soiled by sin. The Church is holy because it is on a holy mission. It is fighting the good fight, and is filled with the Holy Spirit to enable that fight to go on.

A mature person is neither a total pessimist nor a naive optimist, but looks at the whole picture. You see how things really are, but also how things *can be*. You see the real faults in yourself, in others, and in the world, but you also see the great potential in yourself, in others, and in the world.

The Church is holy in this sense because it helps us see both what we are and what we can be. The Church doesn't whitewash the human condition. It says boldly, "We are all sinners. We are lost in the dark and need someone to rescue us." But the Church also says, "We are all sons and daughters of the living God. We were created to be no less than the radiant inhabitants of heaven. Let us be all that we can be in the power of God, leaving behind the works of darkness and moving forward together into the full and abundant life that he has promised."

THE CATHOLIC CHURCH

The Universal Corner Shop

If you want to discover the reality of the Catholic Church, you don't have to travel all the way to Rome; that's simply where the international headquarters are. Instead, discover your neighborhood Catholic parish church. There, in your own town, the one universal community of Christ's disciples has its local branch.

In your local Catholic parish the ancient, universal Church that Christ founded becomes real. There you will meet people who are struggling to fight the battle against evil and who are also seeking to follow Christ. Just as marriage makes love real, so joining the Catholic Church makes real your commitment to Christ. When something is real it is both difficult and glorious. So it is with marriage and with being a Catholic. It is tough. It is a challenge. But then, did you expect the Christian life to be easy?

Here, There, and Everywhere

One good definition of the word *catholic* is "universal." In other words, the Catholic Church is everywhere. It is not tied down to one particular region, country, or ethnic group. Over the centuries, by the power of the Holy Spirit, the Catholic community has permeated every continent. People have become Catholics from virtually every tribe, nationality, and race on earth.

As a result, there is a huge variety within the Catholic Church. If you go to South America or Africa, you will find poor Catholics living in simple communities. They might worship in a church that is no more than a shed. Their music will be simple ethnic music, and their prayers will be the prayers of the poor.

On the other hand, if you visit an affluent suburb in the United States or in Europe, you will find relatively wealthy Catholics in comfortable, modern churches or exquisite ancient cathedrals. Their struggle is to follow Christ despite having so much material wealth. Their challenge is to make generous sacrifices of both prayer and money to help their poor brothers and sisters in other parts of the world.

Contrasts like these can be multiplied over and over again. East and west, north and south, rich and poor, educated and un-educated, black and white, men and women, old people and chil-dren — in the Catholic Church they all exist together as the family of God.

Believing in a universal Church does not simply mean believ-ing with our heads that such a worldwide family exists; it also means that we believe with our hearts that we *belong* to that fam-ily. It means that we become a living part of the vast and complex community of followers of Jesus Christ around the world and down through the ages.

Salvation Outside the Church?

It is a wonderful thing to belong to a family of people who are united in one faith, following one Lord, and belonging to one church. But being a Catholic also means that we are members of the Body of Christ. As such, we have a new power in our lives. We share in the same power that raised Jesus from the dead. Because we share in this power, we are delivered from eternal death and have the promise of eternal life with God.

Is that unfair to all those who are not Catholics? In the section on "one Church" I explained that all non-Catholic Christians who have faith in Christ, and who have been baptized into his death and resurrection, can also share in the hope of salvation.

But what about the many people who follow religions other than Christianity? Are they able to be saved, or are they already damned?

There is also the question of all those who have never heard about Jesus Christ. Will God send them all to hell simply because they have never had the chance to have faith in Christ and be baptized? If so, it sounds very unfair.

Christianity Pure and Simple

Denial and Affirmation

Catholics recognize the goodness and truth in other religions. We recognize that the Jews, for example, are our older brothers and sisters in the faith. Jesus was a Jew. Christianity grew out of the Jewish religion. Catholics believe that a Jewish person's faith would be fulfilled and completed if he were to become a Christian, but we also recognize that God can draw faithful Jews to himself if it is his will. If he does so it is through Jesus Christ's victory over death.

For another example, Catholics also recognize that Muslims seek to follow the same God as Christians and Jews. Muslims follow the teachings of Mohammed as written in the Koran. We don't agree with everything they teach, and they certainly don't agree with everything that Catholics believe.

However, despite our disagreements, there is much that we can agree on, and there is much that we can praise within the Islamic religion. In fact, Catholics believe in goodness, truth, and beauty wherever it is found. Thus we realize that all other religions aren't 100 percent wrong. Instead we believe that the other world religions are good as far as they go, but that they are only a preparation for the fullness for God's truth as shown in Jesus Christ. In the other religions the truth is understood in a partial way. In Jesus Christ the truth has come in all its fullness.

Catholics are able to affirm these good things in other religions without denying the truths we hold to as Catholics. We are able to fight beside them in the battle against evil while helping them to fight it more effectively by sharing with them the full truth about what Jesus has done for us.

As for salvation, we know that God sent Jesus to save the world, not to condemn it. We pray that through Jesus' death and resurrection all people might be saved, and we trust God to answer this prayer in his own way.

Us and Them

Christianity remains the largest world religion, but there are many other religions besides the Muslims and Jews. We can see how a Muslim or a Jew, who claims to worship the same God as Christians do, might be closer to Christianity than people of other faiths. We might wonder what happens to Buddhists, Sikhs, Bahá'is, Hindus, pagans, animists, and so forth. They don't profess to worship the same God as the Christians. In the Gospel, Jesus says clearly that he is the only way to God the Father. If those who follow other religions do not believe in Jesus, can they be saved?

A Universal Mission

The Catholic Church is the universal Church, and that means that it has a universal mission. Before he went back to heaven Jesus commanded his followers to go into the whole world to proclaim the good news. He wanted everyone to be set free from their selfishness to attain a new and abundant life.

Catholics want to learn from non-Christian religions. We want to claim what is good in them and endorse all that is true and beautiful in their teachings. However, we are also aware that the Catholic system is the only one that is truly universal. In other words, all that is good, beautiful, and true within all the other religions can also be found within the Catholic faith.

If you knew someone who was digging a trench with a teaspoon, you might applaud his efforts. You could acknowledge that he was doing an excellent job as far as his skill and his tools could allow. But if you had a spade or a bulldozer, you would want to tell him about the even better tools that you had available, so that he could dig a better ditch in a fraction of the time.

This is how Catholics feel about Jesus' command to tell others the good news. For those who have never heard the news, the commandment is simple: tell everyone that God loves them and Jesus has come to set them free from selfishness and final death.

It *is* possible for a person of non-Christian faith to find salvation; but it will be the salvation won for them by Jesus Christ, whether they realize it or not. And that salvation is so much simpler and more rewarding to pursue by its right name. For those who follow other religions, the process is like telling the person who is using a teaspoon to dig a ditch that there is a better, fuller way to complete the task.

Redeeming the Whole World

This is why the Catholic Church will always be a missionary church. Every Catholic — whether a layperson or a priest, bishop, monk, or nun — is called to tell others the good news about Jesus Christ.

Our mission is to do nothing less than transform the world. Jesus died and rose again to set loose the power to effect that transformation. We, as his Body on earth today, are required to carry on his work and complete the job he gave us to do.

Each of us must get on with the job in the way best suited to our own personalities, gifts, and abilities. Some will help to redeem the world by telling people about Jesus Christ and by helping them to have faith and come to be baptized.

Others will be busy transforming the world through political activity, or through education, health care, or social work. Others transform the world by bringing up many children who are on fire with the love of God. Still others will work to transform the whole world by giving their lives to prayer and worship.

No matter what our particular task, each of us is called to transform the world by first being transformed ourselves. Do you want others to know the joy, the power, and the confidence that come from having faith in Christ? Then show them the proof in your own transformed life.

The command to go out into the world and transform it by his power was the last word Jesus gave to his Apostles. They bore his word and his power into the world; and we take part in the same mission because we share in the same faith that has been given to us by those very same Apostles two thousand years ago.

THE APOSTOLIC CHURCH

A Firm Foundation

Jesus told a story about two men who built houses. The first man found a cheap piece of sandy ground and put up a nice house quite easily. The second man invested in a rocky piece of high ground. It was hard work to build the house in such a place, but the foundation was firm and sure. When the floods and rains came, the man who had built on sand saw his house fall down, while the man who had built on rock was safe and secure.

Later in the New Testament, Paul says that the Church is built on the foundation of the prophets and Apostles. What he means is that the community of Christians is like the second man's house. It is built carefully and with much hard work on a solid and sure foundation. The belief, worship, and work of Christians are rooted in the life and ministry of Jesus' first followers.

Jesus had many followers and disciples, but from them he chose twelve for a special ministry of leadership. These twelve are called *Apostles*, which means "ambassadors" or "sent ones." Jesus gave the Apostles authority to continue his work. He said that he was sending them just as God had sent him: into the world to proclaim a saving message. He also promised to be with them forever and to send the Holy Spirit to guide and strengthen them.

Therefore, when Jesus ascended into heaven, he left behind a group of men who would be his agents. As he was the hand of God, they would be his hands, his feet, his voice on earth. In the Gospels we find that the Apostles were given power to do what Jesus had done, in three ways: power to teach the truth faithfully; power over the forces of evil, illness, and death; and power to forgive sins in Jesus' name.

The Successors of the Apostles

The Acts of the Apostles in the New Testament tells us how these "sent ones" got on with the job. The story opens with the day of Pentecost. The Apostles were gathered with the other followers of Jesus, wondering what would happen next. Suddenly the Holy Spirit came upon them in a glorious rush, and they received power for the task that Jesus had given them.

The apostle Peter emerged as their natural leader. He preached to crowds of people about Jesus, and thousands responded to the good news, believed in Jesus, and were baptized.

Eventually a prominent Jew named Paul was converted and joined the Apostles. He was the first apostle of the next generation. Through a powerful conversion experience, he also claimed to have been chosen by Christ, and his calling was confirmed by the other Apostles. Together Peter and Paul helped to establish the Church.

The other apostles went into the whole known world spreading the good news and starting local churches wherever they went. Before long, throughout the Roman Empire, little groups of Christians were meeting in homes and local halls. The new little religion prospered and grew. Churches flourished, and soon in the major cities there were many little cells of believers in Jesus Christ. The apostles appointed leaders in each city, and it was natural for the leader appointed by the apostles to become the leader of all the Christians in that city and surrounding area.

Jesus had promised to be with his followers forever, and the first generation of Christians realized that, after the death of the Apostles, the power Jesus had given them had been passed on to the local church leaders they had appointed. The idea that leadership could be handed on from one leader to the next generation was a normal part of the culture of the day. As a result the leaders of the local churches (called bishops) were seen to be the natural successors of the Apostles.

Built on the Rock

Paul said that the Church was built on the solid foundation of the prophets and apostles. He must have been thinking of a conversation Jesus had had with Peter. Peter's given name was actually Simon. But when he recognized that Jesus was the Son of God, Jesus responded by praising him and giving him a new name. From then on he was to be called *Peter,* which means "Rock." Then Jesus said, "On this rock I will build my Church."[52]

After he rose from the dead Jesus appointed Peter to the leadership role in a different way. He asked Peter three times to "feed my sheep."[53] Jesus had already said that he was the Good Shepherd, and just before he went back to heaven he delegated to Peter his job as head Shepherd on earth.

Peter emerged as the natural leader after Jesus' return to heaven. Eventually he went to Rome and, with Paul, helped establish the Church in the empire's capital city. The leaders of the Roman church were therefore seen to be the successors of Peter. Because

[52] Matthew 6:18.
[53] Cf. John 21:15, 16, 17.

he was the leader of the twelve Apostles it was natural that his successors — the leaders of the Roman church — were also seen to be the leaders of the whole Church.

Catholics believe that there is still a successor of Peter active in the world today. The present-day Bishop of Rome is the Pope. The word *Pope* simply means "Papa." The Pope is our spiritual father on earth. He speaks today with the same voice of authority that Jesus gave to Peter two thousand years ago.

Reliable Leadership

It is impossible for any organization to prosper without proper leadership. It is impossible for any army to win a war without a supreme commander. Likewise, the Church cannot have unity if it is not united under one leader. Jesus the Good Shepherd said that there would be, "one flock and one shepherd." He asked Peter to be that shepherd. We believe Peter's successor still plays the same unifying leadership role today.

The Pope is not an all-powerful absolute monarch. The New Testament shows that Peter ruled by consulting the other Apostles and deciding on matters together with them. Likewise, the Pope rules the Church through consultation with all the bishops of the world as well as through their consultation with all the priests and people. Yet it is not a democracy. It is a collaborative and consultative council with a clear leader at the top and a clear chain of command.

Jesus promised his followers that the Holy Spirit, the "Spirit of Truth," would come to them. In this way Jesus guaranteed to his followers a measure of his own ability to teach the truth without error. This same gift resides in the Church today. The bishops of the Church maintain, defend, develop, and teach the same truth that has been handed down to them from the Apostles. Because of this historical truth, we can rely on the Church to teach the truth about Jesus without error.

Written Answers

The teaching of the Catholic Church is rooted in the faith, life, and ministry of the Apostles. They were granted authority by Jesus himself. We believe that the Church today teaches with that same authority and is empowered by the same Holy Spirit.

One of the fruits of the Church's power to understand and teach the truth is the Bible. The Bible is a collection of Jewish and Christian religious writings. The Christians of the first few centuries gathered the stories of Jesus, and the letters that the Apostles had written to the churches. They gathered the history of the Apostles' lives and some other writings. Eventually they recognized that the Holy Spirit had actually helped the human authors write some of these unique witnesses to Jesus Christ.

These writings were then granted special Church approval as the Holy Scriptures or the Bible. The Bible then became a unique source book for further teachings. The leaders of the Church realized that the words of the Bible put them in intimate contact with the teachings of the Apostles, and therefore with Jesus himself. The Scriptures gave them a firm guideline and measuring rod for the truth. Nothing they would preach or teach could ever contradict the meaning of what was taught in the Bible. If it did, they were wrong and not the Bible.

In addition to the written teaching of the Apostles there was an unwritten body of teaching. The preachers and teachers of one generation handed down the teachings of the Apostles in oral form. The Catholic Church maintains the apostolic tradition as another branch of authoritative apostolic teaching alongside the Bible.

Christianity Pure and Simple

The fullness of the Christian faith is expressed in the historical, full-blooded beliefs of the Catholic Church. These beliefs have been fully presented most recently in a book called the *Catechism of the Catholic Church*. This is a scholarly but readable and inspiring text that draws together the truths of the Bible and the truths of Christian tradition to express clearly what Catholics believe.

The *Catechism* is a clear collection of Catholic beliefs, but Catholic beliefs are not just "book knowledge." The Bible and the oral tradition of the Church are rooted in the living experience of the people of God. The Bible and the tradition complement each other, and come alive as the Bible is read within the daily and weekly worship of the Church. It is good to read the Bible on our own, but we must always be aware that the Bible on its own can be interpreted in many ways. Like statistics, it can mean almost anything to anybody. That is why Catholics always read the Bible in the context of the ongoing traditions of the Church. In that way, the Church that gave us the Bible also helps us to understand the Bible correctly.

Authority Without Authoritarianism

We saw earlier that there are about twenty thousand non-Catholic Christian denominations in the United States. The reason there are so many different groups is that the leaders of these groups have all disagreed among themselves.

They disagree because they have looked only to the Bible for their source book, and they have read the Bible outside the context of the Church. The Bible alone does not have the authority to teach us without error. If it did, there would not be twenty thousand non-Catholic denominations — each one of which claims to be really following the Bible!

172

When we say that the Catholic faith is apostolic, we mean that we follow the faith of the Apostles as expressed in the Bible, but we also believe that the Holy Spirit who inspired those Apostles is still alive today. That Spirit works through the Church's teaching ministry. The Pope and the bishops of the Church are the successors of the Apostles and are empowered to teach us how to understand the Christian faith in all its fullness. And we further believe that the Pope has been given the special grace of *infallibility*.

Now, when we say the Pope is infallible, we simply mean that when it comes to teaching matters of faith and morals (and only then), the Pope has been given the gift to teach us God's truths without error. This doesn't mean the Pope is a sinless person or that he never makes mistakes in ordinary areas of human opinion. It doesn't mean that he is all-knowing or that he channels God's words through his mouth. It simply means that when he does teach and proclaim for the hearing of all the Church, what he teaches will be reliable and true. This ensures the integrity of Christ's teachings over time.

PRIVILEGES AND DUTIES

Where There's a Will There's a Way

Because the Church is one, holy, catholic, and apostolic we have a clear responsibility as members of the Church. As individuals, we also have a duty to be one, holy, catholic, and apostolic.

These four descriptions of the Church help us to understand our goal and destiny as Christians. I am called as an individual to follow the faith that was first taught by the Apostles and has been handed down to me through the ages.

The apostolic faith is found in the Bible, but it is also available to you through the continued teaching and preaching of the

Church. During Mass the priest gives a homily that helps you to understand how the apostolic faith applies to your life today.

Bishops regularly issue pastoral letters that help maintain, defend, and apply the apostolic faith. The Pope writes and publishes encyclical letters that also address particular concerns and help to apply the apostolic faith in the world today.

Finally, there is a wealth of Catholic material that helps to teach the apostolic faith. Books, television stations, videos, pamphlets, music, and websites all keep the apostolic faith alive and help you understand it and apply it better.

For Better or for Worse

The apostolic faith includes not only the religious truths about Jesus Christ and the Church, but also the teaching on how Christians should live.

Catholics have been blamed in the past for focusing too much on sin and making people feel guilty for what they've done wrong. It is true that some Catholic leaders have done this in an overly aggressive, even sour way. However, it is part of the Church's duty to show us where we're going wrong, just as it is a doctor's duty to diagnose a serious illness correctly.

The doctor diagnoses cancer not because he wants you to die, but because he wants you to get better. It is the same when the Church points out where our lives are going wrong. Church teachers and ministers have the courage to tell us what is wrong not because they want us to feel bad, but because they want us to get better.

Being a Christian means that we are constantly aware of our failings, but it also means we are constantly aware of God's help in our lives. Christians are keenly alert to their failures because they are so keenly alert to how much better life can be.

A Wider Vision

As we are called to follow the apostolic faith as individuals, we are also called to practice a *universal* faith. Being a Christian is not just about me and God or even about me and God and my local community. It is about me and God and the whole universe.

Being Catholic puts my own little life in perspective. My personality, my race, and my nationality are all part of a much wider family that includes every other background in the world. As such, I am responsible for these other Christians, and they are responsible for me. To be Catholic means that I must get involved in the lives of others. I must respect others sexually. No man or woman can be regarded as a mere sex toy. Neither can I exploit or use people by cheating them, stealing from them, or abusing them in any way. From now on every person is my brother or my sister.

This worldwide vision of my place in relationship with the whole of humanity affects other aspects of my life, too. I must care for the poor, the disabled, refugees, political prisoners, and the oppressed. God might call me to give my life in service to these poor and outcast brothers and sisters of mine, or he might simply enable me to support others who work to help those who are less well off.

I cannot be complacent. My life is no longer my own. It has been given to me so that I may help my brothers and sisters in this universal family of God called the Catholic Church.

Be Perfect as Your Father in Heaven Is Perfect

Jesus actually told his Apostles that they should be perfect as God is perfect. Talk about setting high standards! What Jesus meant by this is that those of us who are members of the one, holy, catholic, and apostolic Church are called not only to follow the apostolic faith, and not only to have a universal outlook, but to strive after real holiness.

Every day of our life should now have a new goal: we are taking a further step toward that wholeness, or holiness, that God has designed us to attain. This means that every word, action, thought, and decision must be focused on this aim.

This activity is empowered by the Holy Spirit, and the Holy Spirit's power is delivered to us through the ministry of the Church. Once we see that this is the goal, all the other dos and don'ts of religion take their proper place. All the guidelines and commandments that the Church gives us are seen suddenly as means to an end, not as ends in themselves. In the same way, the sacraments of the Church cease to be religious duties and become events in which we receive the power to live the Christian life and are transformed from within into better images of Christ himself.

If we are called to be wholly holy, then the rules and disciplines of the religious life become as joyful and difficult for us as an athlete's training program. An athlete doesn't mind getting up early and keeping to a strict diet and a grueling regime of exercise, because he has his eyes set on the goal. He knows what he wants to achieve, and the training is merely the tool to get there.

It is the same in the religious life. To be holy requires discipline in prayer, in self-sacrifice, in study, and in a constant check on our selfish instincts. This regime can become legalistic and sour, but it is meant to be as liberating and life-giving as the athlete's training. Remember, running a race is exhilarating as well as exhausting; and an adventure may be dangerous, but it is also exciting.

That They May Be One

In his last hours Jesus prayed that his followers, "might be one as you and I, Father, are one."[54] In other words, Jesus wanted them

[54]Cf. John 17:22.

to be one with him, but he also wanted them to be one with each other, and one within themselves.

We follow the apostolic faith, we maintain a universal outlook, and we strive and train for holiness because we are seeking this essential unity of being. We want to be one within ourselves. We want to be one with each other. We want to be one with the whole of creation. We want to be one with God.

We begin to share in this unity through our worship in the Catholic Church. We make a commitment to attend Mass every week because that is where we get refocused. At Mass the unity we long for actually exists — even if it is still imperfect. At Mass we join ourselves with Christ, with our Christian brothers and sisters, and with God. *Communion* actually means "union with" or "union across," and so at Mass that union which will one day have an eternal dimension is made immediately real to us.

Transformation Starts at Home

Staying in touch with Christ, and then spreading his life and love throughout the world, leads to a final goal. We are actually called to a higher and greater destiny than any of us can imagine. We are destined to become the very sons and daughters of God. Each one of us, with all our sadness, failures, and regrets, is called to total redemption and transformation. Jesus Christ wants us to be made into his likeness and to share the radiance of his glory.

The beauty of the Christian faith is that this glory is not found in the things that appear high and mighty. The glory is found instead in the things that are lowly and humble. The fact that God's son came to be born in a drafty stable says it all. The glory of heaven is always expressed in the simplicity of ordinary life.

Therefore, if we want to be transformed into the radiant glory of Christ, we don't begin by striving for high and holy religious experiences. We don't attempt great feats of prayer, abstinence, and self-denial. We don't lock ourselves away to pursue a purified spiritual existence. Instead we get on with ordinary life — but now in an extraordinary way.

Christ's glory shining out of the ordinary life of a carpenter in Nazareth two thousand years ago reminds us that it is in our ordinary tasks, trials, and tribulations that our transformation will take place. So be ordinary in an extraordinary way. Connect with Christ in the ordinary, sometimes boring glory of Mass every week. See the chance to be like Christ by getting up early to make the breakfast, helping others even when they don't ask, and living a life of simple sacrifice every day.

It is by being who we are meant to be that we are transformed beyond ourselves. It is by following Christ in our everyday lives that we become like him, and it is through a lifetime of this simple spiritual life that we are able to transform the whole world.

FURTHER UP AND FURTHER IN

The Long and Winding Road

The spiritual way is not the easiest path through life. Jesus said the way was narrow and there are few who find it. On the other hand, he said the way to spiritual destruction was a broad downward slope. It is easy to slide into hell. It is difficult to climb into heaven.

Is anything good ever easy? What great thing has ever been done overnight? It is true that we are called to a glory beyond our imagining. It is true that we are called to be radiant and everlasting beings — no less than sons and daughters of God himself. But it is also true that we have a long way to go.

But when you think about it, is there really anything else worth living for? Physical pleasure fades. Money is good only in this life;

they don't put pockets in shrouds. Status and fame disappear; all those who remember you also die. Even our dearest human loves will be snatched away by illness and death. Our only hope is to be united with all that we love in a greater reality beyond the grave. The spiritual life, therefore, not only leads to a happier existence here, but also offers the only hope for a happier existence on the other side of death.

That happy existence is not guaranteed simply because we happen to want it. Jesus Christ has opened up the way to eternal life. He has given it to us as a gift, but that treasure must be sought and found. The treasure is free, but we must study the map and go on the long journey to find it. Living our lives for this end is the best investment we can ever make.

*We Move Further Up and
Further Into God's Glory*
The glorious thing about following the spiritual path is that every day we are making further progress toward all that we have ever loved and longed for in life. Every path leads somewhere, and if we are following the way of Christ, then he is more than the way; he is also the destination.

Heaven is not simply a happy place on the other side of the clouds where we will see all our loved ones once again. Heaven is the fulfillment of all our hopes and dreams. It is a reality that makes everything on this earth seem like a dream.

Some people say you make your own heaven and hell here on earth. This is true in one sense, but it is more true to say that you are choosing between heaven or hell every day here on earth. You are choosing heaven or hell because every day — indeed every moment — you are choosing whether you wish to live God's way or your way. If you wish to live God's way, then that way will logically lead to God. If you choose to live your way, then your choice naturally leads away from God.

To choose heaven, therefore, is not a "once and done" choice. It is a "once and done over and over again" choice.

Will we choose to connect with Jesus at Mass and Confession, or will we ignore him? Will we choose to give our money and time to a just cause, or will we spend our resources solely for our own pleasure? Will we give of ourselves for the good of others or simply pursue our own desires? Down one route lies heaven. Down the other, hell.

The Slippery Slope

Is there such a place as hell? Will people really be tormented forever with pain and fire? It is not pleasant to think about hell, but when you do think about it, it becomes clear that hell is a necessity. If heaven is a place of goodness and justice, then there must be a place for all those who, all their lives, have run from all that is good, true, and just.

Does God send people to hell? It is more likely that he simply gives each of us what we've always wanted. If some people flee from God all their lives, can we imagine that they would actually *want* to go to heaven? They would flee from the intensity of his presence, and the place they would prefer must be hell.

Perhaps then it is simply the case that the light of God is the same light to those who are saved and those who are damned. The only difference is that for those who have always loved goodness, truth, and beauty, the light will be the light of Christ, while for those who have always loved evil, the same light will be experienced as the searing flames of hell.

Whatever hell consists of, we can say that it must be the everlasting torture of being left alone without God, without love, without beauty, without goodness, and without truth. If we have choice, then we must have the choice to go there. If we do any action that, by its very nature, takes us away from God, and if we persist in that action without ever acknowledging that we are wrong, we are in danger of ending up with the fruit of that action — and that fruit is a future cut off from God, from life, and from love.

The Third Way

Talking about heaven and hell in such black-and-white terms makes people uncomfortable. In one sense there is nothing wrong with that. Hell is meant to be uncomfortable, and the best sermon ever preached about hell consists of only two words: "Fear hell."

But people are also uncomfortable because we all realize that things are not so black and white. Each one of us might long for heaven, but we also stumble and fall into our darker desires, laziness, and selfishness. The eternal state of each one of our hearts is not so clear-cut.

If we are honest, we admit that we are not saintly enough to go straight to heaven, but we also hope that we are not wicked enough to head for hell. To see ourselves this way is not proud or unduly humble. It is just realistic.

This is why the Church teaches that there is a place called purgatory, a place of purgation or cleansing. Everybody in purgatory will eventually make it to heaven. It's just that they need some time to get their act together. If you like, purgatory is a place to wash up before mealtime. It is a place where our failures, imperfections, and faults can continue to be put right by the help of God's gift of grace. As long as we have sought God's way in this life, as long as we have put our trust in Christ's saving work, we can have a confident hope that after we have been cleaned up we will enter into the final glory of God's presence.

All Shall Be Well

This final hope is the glory and joy of all Christians. We do not simply wish for pie in the sky and a happy hunting ground after we pass on. Instead heaven is the fulfillment of all things. There, all that is divided shall be one. There, all that was soiled and impure shall be holy and wholly itself. There, all that was small and narrow-minded will be universal in its scope and vision.

The vision of heaven in the New Testament has the Apostles and prophets on thrones around the throne of God. This is a symbolic way of saying that heaven will be a fulfillment of all that the Church hints at here on earth. The welcome home we receive when we become Catholics is just a hint of the greater welcome home we shall receive on our entrance into heaven.

Heaven will be like a great family reunion or a vast wedding feast. Everyone will be gathered in the unity and peace for which they were created. At that point the transformation of every soul will be complete. Each one of us will be fully and wholly ourselves because we will have found our rightful place in the everlasting life of Christ.

We will know then as we are known. We will see that all is well; that we fit into a destiny for the universe far more wonderful and beautiful than we ever could have imagined.

Additional Reading

The Catechism of the Catholic Church

CHRISTIAN CLASSICS

Mere Christianity, by C. S. Lewis
The Screwtape Letters, by C. S. Lewis
Orthodoxy, by G. K. Chesterton
The Everlasting Man, by G. K. Chesterton
The Creed in Slow Motion, by Ronald Knox
Early Christian Writings, by Maxwell Staniforth
The Penguin Dictionary of Saints, by Donald Attwater and
  Catherine Rachel Jones

MODERN CATHOLIC BOOKS

Catholic Lives, by Greg Watts: a collection of stories of people
  who have become Catholic.
The Path to Rome, by Dwight Longenecker: a more weighty collection of conversion stories than *Catholic Lives*.
More Christianity, by Dwight Longenecker: a friendly explanation of the Catholic faith for non-Catholic Christians.
Adventures in Orthodoxy, by Dwight Longenecker: a witty and
  colorful exploration of Christian belief.

Christianity Pure and Simple

Exploring the Catholic Church, by Marcellino D'Ambrosio: a good
brief introduction to the Catholic Church today.

What Catholics Really Believe, by Karl Keating: an exploration of
the Catholic faith in a question-and-answer format.

Surprised by Truth, Surprised by Truth 2, and *Surprised by Truth 3*,
by Patrick Madrid: three volumes of American conversion
stories.

Dwight Longenecker

Dwight Longenecker is an American who has lived in England for over twenty years. A former Anglican priest whose conversion to Catholicism appears in *Surprised by Truth 3*, he writes regularly for many magazines, newspapers, and journals in Britain, Ireland, and the United States.

Longenecker is the editor of a collection of British conversion stories called *The Path to Rome — Modern Journeys to the Catholic Faith* (Gracewing, 1999) and the author of *St. Benedict and St. Thérèse* (Gracewing/Our Sunday Visitor, 2002), *More Christianity* (Our Sunday Visitor, 2002) and *Adventures in Orthodoxy* (Sophia Institute Press, 2002). He has also written a series of evangelical booklets for the Catholic Truth Society, which formed the basis for this book.

As well as being a writer, Longenecker is an accomplished public speaker and broadcaster. He and his wife, Alison, have four children.

Sophia Institute Press®

Sophia Institute® is a nonprofit institution that seeks to restore man's knowledge of eternal truth, including man's knowledge of his own nature, his relation to other persons, and his relation to God. Sophia Institute Press® serves this end in numerous ways. It publishes translations of foreign works to make them accessible to English-speaking readers, it brings back into print books that have been long out of print, and it publishes important new books that fulfill the ideals of Sophia Institute®. These books afford readers a rich source of the enduring wisdom of mankind. Sophia Institute Press® makes these high-quality books available to the public by using advanced technology and by soliciting donations to subsidize its publishing costs.

Your generosity can help provide the public with editions of works containing the enduring wisdom of the ages. Please send your tax-deductible contribution to the address below.

For your free catalog,
Call toll-free: 1-800-888-9344

Sophia Institute Press®
Box 5284
Manchester, NH 03108
www.sophiainstitute.com

Sophia Institute® is a tax-exempt institution as defined by the Internal Revenue Code, Section 501(c)(3). Tax I.D. 22-2548708.